Glenna,
Thanks for your
help!
Sharon Hamfn

1

Thriving Beyond Cancer

By Sharon Henifin CLC, CN-BA
With Michelle Cameron MD, PT, MCR

Copyright 2017 by Sharon Henifin CLC, CN-BA
Published by Butterfly Books

ISBN-13:
978-1544049182

ISBN-10:
1544049188
Printed in the United States of America

Cover Design by Sharon Henifin

Publisher's Cataloging
Henifin, Sharon
        Thriving Beyond Cancer / Sharon Henifin
        ISBN 13: 978-1544049182

        1. Cancer
        2. Self Help
        3. Psychology
        4. Women's Issues

Dedication

"Just when the caterpillar thought her world was over...she became a butterfly."—unknown

Just imagine...an insect that crawls on the ground that is barely noticed can be transformed into a new life. A life that is more colorful, graceful and elegant than before. The time comes in all of our lives where we find our wings and fly. When we accept the wings we are given, where flight is effortless and beautiful for the entire world to see.

I create hope and healing for those dealing with life circumstances. Transforming lives and I will help you realign your focus on what's important so you can live your best life.

This book is dedicated to all the women I have had the privilege to meet, to become familiar with on an intimate level and for the ladies who shared their stories with me and gave me their permission to use them in this publication. I feel honored and blessed to have shared their cancer journey and beyond by creating a safe place as they traversed from patient to survivor to thriving beyond cancer.

I also want to thank several people for their help with this book. Michelle Cameron kept me moving forward, verified the medical information and did initial edits. Kathlene Kelley, Glenna Weixel, Kate Loftus, Lauri Nelson, Becky Olson and Allison Hancock, Yvonne Nydigger and Chris Parker for their perspectives and edits.

Thriving Beyond Cancer
By Sharon Henifin

Table of Contents

Introduction

There is no easy "how-to" book to manage a cancer diagnosis, treatment, and navigate the journey back. This book offers validation for you're feeling and gives a voice to those emotions and scary emotions, some you haven't yet felt and others you'd rather not admit. My hope is that you will find tools in this book helpful. My goal is for you to embrace who you are now and move closer to living your best life in the future.

No matter what your treatment choices have been, you have experienced a physical and emotional battlefield. You have been brave to endure those surgeries and therapies. Give yourself credit for your courage and the willingness to forge ahead through this unknown playing field. There are those who choose not to take that path and have paid the ultimate price for their decision.

We are much more resilient than we give ourselves credit for. When something like a cancer diagnosis hits us, or someone we love, at first it seems as if we will never be able to endure it. Yet most of us move through this tough time and return to levels of happiness even higher than before this health crisis.

The purpose of this book is to validate each woman's feelings as she finishes her treatment of this deadly disease. When the doctor dismisses her after months of close scrutiny, it feels as if the medical rug has been yanked out from under her. For others peoples' comfort, she has spent months minimizing what she had managed. She stuffed her emotions to endure the difficult lifesaving medical treatments, and then finds when her doctor appointments slow, those unprocessed emotions, plus anxiety for the future, bubble up. After seeing her mortality, she realizes her life is ill-fitting. With modern medical advances women are living longer after cancer but finding their values have changed. What once was important seems insignificant. Although this is a weighty topic, I have spun it in a warm and loving way, validating common concerns and delivering the tools needed to transition from patient to survivor to thriver.

There are several shelves of cancer books, but the emotional journey of cancer survivorship and the issues surrounding them are rarely addressed and few books are designed to answer how to move past the fear and lingering side effects into life after cancer. This book fills the gap and takes it to the next level with thrivership. It provides hope to women and their families. Thrivership encourages much more than surviving the disease, it empowers the readers to dream and contemplate how to combine their natural gifts and talents with their passions and move into their next chapter. I discuss the lasting nature of treatment side effects and how to deal with them, physically and emotionally. I encourage the reader to differentiate what they have control over from and what they do not. I tackle the tough subject of advanced disease, everyone's nightmare, demystifying and bringing hope for the chronic side of cancer as well as death and dying pieces missing in most other cancer survivor books. This book incorporates survivor quotes and stories, as well as my own story as a survivor, my skills as a life coach and my experiences as Cofounder of Breast Friends, an emotional support organization.

I understand the need for the emotional and physical transition from patient to survivor and then to thriver. I was diagnosed with breast cancer in 1993 and will give you more details about that throughout this book. I have worked with women dealing with something similar since I healed from my own reconstructive surgery. I work with cancer patients and their families at Breast Friends, www.breastfriends.org, an Oregon nonprofit organization I co-founded in 2000. I have had the pleasure to work with thousands of cancer patients during their journey. God has blessed me with the gifts to intuitively understand people, a positive energy, enthusiasm, and willingness to help inspire patients to embrace the cancer treatment and give them the tools they need to move beyond the cancer experience.

I became a certified professional life coach in 2008. This started a new chapter in my life, giving me tools to help women transition from a victim mentality to thriver. I started offering workshops and retreats designed to use life coaching techniques to help patients move through the cancer journey. These workshops are for women who have finished their formal cancer treatment and feel stuck. Like me, I've found many women don't know how to rebuild their lives after cancer. Many struggle to reach beyond this life altering experience to live their best, most fulfilling, life. These workshops were the catalyst to write this book.

Prologue

When my adopted mom passed away many years ago I made a decision. I vowed to make a difference. I remember walking out of her memorial service feeling great sadness, not so much for her death but for the life she wasted. She lived 76 years on this earth and from my perspective it felt as if she didn't have much to show for it. I'm not talking about personal wealth or possessions; I'm talking about making a difference in the world. I'm not suggesting that everybody travel the world, write a book or be a famous speaker. I am suggesting that it is our responsibility to use the gifts we've been given to be our best self. My mom was an unhappy person, not grateful for what she had, and her bitterness permeated her existence.

We have all been dealt difficult situations, tragedy, and challenges. How we transcend these obstacles makes us stronger and more resilient. Working through the emotions and moving past experiences in life helps us discover our strengths. Don't waste your time and energy dwelling on the past or the negative. Just like other challenges, I believe it's important to acknowledge what you've been through and then move forward. That's the first step and what this book is designed to help you accomplish. If you are feeling stuck in the patient mode, keep reading for the perspectives of others and the tools to rediscover the joy your deserve.

Part 1

Chapter 1

Cancer Changes Everything

A few days after my 40th birthday, I felt a weird pain shooting through my left breast. I started poking where the pain seemed to originate, trying to reduce its intensity. That's when I felt it, a small, hard pea-sized lump in my breast. I checked on it for a couple of days hoping it was no longer there. When it hadn't gone away I decided I better have it examined. I made an appointment with the plastic surgeon that had done my breast augmentation surgery 14 years earlier. I was a 34 B with augmentation so you can imagine how flat I was before that. I remember lying down on the examination table, scared but hopeful, while my doctor conducted a thorough clinical breast exam. I listened intently to his words. "It's probably nothing, but let's get it out of there just in case." The problem was, as I peered into his warm caring eyes while he spoke and I realized his eyes didn't match his words. His eyes told me I was in deep trouble.

That was a Tuesday and the following Tuesday I was to go to the hospital day surgery unit to have that mystery lump removed. I was very anxious about going into surgery as I'm sure we all are. Part of me was excited to have this hard mass removed from my body as soon as possible, yet at the same time, I was afraid my greatest fears would be confirmed. It's funny how such a seemingly small thing can change your life forever.

Before finding the lump my connection to cancer was limited. Cancer was for "old" people, like my aunt who died when I was a kid. I remember people whispering about how she had another surgery or had to endure the next treatment. This was in the 60's when people didn't say the word cancer out loud, it was called the C word, or they didn't name it at all. Come to find out she had been diagnosed with breast cancer, but again this was before they spoke about breasts too. Was I going to die from this disease like she did?

About the time I got my news, my mother-in-law developed her second recurrence of breast cancer. This time, unfortunately, it had metastasized to her liver, lungs, and bones. Her pain near the end controlled only with liquid morphine. She spent most of her last months in bed. She was losing her battle while I was starting mine. Could that be my fate?

Just a few weeks before my diagnosis, school started and my youngest had become friends with another fourth grader whose mom had passed away from breast cancer a few years before. Her dad was left to raise both her and her sister alone. Was I going to die from this disease like she did? These were my thoughts, but also the concerns my daughter had as well.

I was officially diagnosed with breast cancer ten days after turning 40 years old in 1993. After I got the news that the lump was indeed cancerous, my doctor also explained that he hadn't gotten clear margins. The crazy world of cancer vernacular had started. There were so many terms I didn't completely understand. I did comprehend one thing, no clear margins meant, I needed more surgery, and I needed it now. So the following Tuesday, seven days after my lumpectomy, I headed back into surgery for a mastectomy.

This time, the lead surgeon was an oncology surgeon, Dr Imatani. He did the mastectomy and Dr. Marshall, my plastic surgeon, placed the expander under the muscle for my reconstruction. I remember lying on the table, frightened and not saying a word. The doctors were preparing me for surgery and suddenly I felt someone's presence behind me. She didn't say a word, but I felt the touch of an angel. I looked up and to my left standing near my head, a nurse had appeared. The gentleness of her touch spoke volumes. She didn't seem to move other than to gently pat and rub my shoulder at the right moment to give me the strength to endure this scary day. I cannot tell you how much that touch, that reassurance, meant to me, even to this day.

The power of touch is healing and restorative. When I'm offering emotional support, I remember my own experience and gently hold my ladies' hands, or pat their leg when appropriate, to add to the power of my words. Sometimes there are no words, but the act of kindness or a simple gesture like touch will say it all.

It's hard to prepare yourself for the shock of having a mastectomy. Bandages cover the worst part, but it still doesn't hide the fact you are flat on that side. I was grateful to at least have the expander in place. Having my reconstruction at the same time as the mastectomy saved me the alarm of seeing my chest concave and an additional surgery. My doctor told me that not only had he removed the lump I had originally felt, but when the pathology of the rest of the breast tissue was examined I had an additional tumor as well. Neither one had been picked up on a mammogram or ultrasound.

After healing from the mastectomy I quickly started chemotherapy. Talk about a deer in the headlights. I could hardly communicate my feelings when I realized the gravity of the situation and what it really meant. Fear overtook me. I felt like a puppet on a string with no control over my own movements or destiny.

When I met with the oncologist I was told that by having my left breast removed my chances of living past five years were about 75%, adding the chemotherapy would take it to around 98%. So, with many years ahead of me to raise my kids and make a difference in this world I opted to add the chemotherapy. In some ways my chemo was much different from the regimes they use today. For the next six months I made trips to the infusion room every two weeks for my IV treatment and I took a daily chemo pill.

Imagining doctors administering poison into my system to improve my chances of survival didn't compute. It never made sense to me, especially at the start of this journey when I felt great. I felt healthy and strong going into chemo but after the steroids wore off I felt crummy for days after chemo. The drugs eventually worked through my system and as I began to regenerate my strength it was time for those nasty chemicals to be put back into my blood stream and then I would feel sick again. After I got into the rhythm of infusions every two weeks, and pills every day, I settled into the pattern and resigned myself to my new reality.

I remember thinking about the old video game of the 80's, Pac Man, and how the little guy was traveling around inside my body the same way he did on the screen. He was on a search and destroy mission scanning my body for any wandering cancer cells that had possibly made it to my bloodstream, my body's superhighway. Even without lymph node involvement, there was a possibility that the cancer had already made that journey which made me nervous. Even though I had a 98% chance to make it to the magic five year mark, there remained a 2% chance that I wouldn't. I made the choice to see it like being pregnant. You are either pregnant or not. You are not 75% pregnant, or 98% pregnant, you either are pregnant or not. So I chose to be cured. I wasn't 98% cured, I was cured.

One thing I remember most about that time is how very lonely I felt. It was a depressing time. I spent way too much time alone, worrying if I would live or die. My family was gone during the day, leaving me for hours to dwell in this scary place in my head. I didn't know anyone my age that had lived through this disease. I didn't know what questions to ask, or what resources were available. I didn't know what I didn't know. So I merely wallowed between the fear and anxiety of cancer and the denial of what I was undergoing.

I hated to watch the changes in my body as well as see the effects of chemotherapy. I felt like I aged overnight after the first chemotherapy threw me into premature menopause. Hot flashes, dry skin, painful intercourse, lowered sex drive; I had all the classic symptoms of a woman in her late 50's and I was only 40. I was angry, but being an amiable people pleaser I didn't know what to do with those emotions, so I stuffed them away to deal with later. I didn't say anything to anyone about how I felt. How could I complain about these quality of life issues when I was fighting for my life? But that didn't change the fact that I felt cheated and miserable.

What Was Next for Me?

When I finished my treatment I tried to get back to my pre-cancer life as quickly as I could. I was raising three kids, and working full time so I thought I knew what was next. However, over the next couple of years I found my life wasn't the same. The things that brought me joy before cancer seemed shallow and unfulfilling. I wanted; no actually, I needed more. My job paid the bills but didn't seem to fill my soul. In fact, I felt I was merely putting in my time until I could retire. My kids were growing up and didn't need me like they once did. I didn't have hobbies that I was passionate about. If someone had asked me, "What do you want?" I'm not sure I had an answer. I just knew that what I had no longer was enough.

Cancer had left me feeling old, vulnerable and tired. The chemotherapy had thrown me into menopause and the hormone therapy I was scheduled to take for five years, kept me in this frustrating state. I couldn't sleep. When I did finally fall asleep, I would have a hot flash, wake up and throw off the covers, fall asleep again, wake up freezing, then repeat, over and over again.

The insomnia itself was difficult as well, waking at 2AM, tossing and turning until about 5:30AM when I needed to get up in less than an hour to start my day. That went on for months until I finally went to the health food store and found a natural method to deal with the hot flashes and even out my hormones. I'm sure my oncologist would have had a hissy fit, but my internist did agree that my quality of life was important. It curbed the hot flashes, at least rounding the peaks and valleys of the roller-coaster. It did however increase my anxiety around the cancer coming back since I did have an estrogen positive tumor and I was adding this natural bit of estrogen-like supplement to my system. This made me hyper vigilant in doing my breast exams on the other side.

Given that neither one of the tumors in my left breast showed up on imaging, I was convinced I also had breast cancer on the other side, but again, I didn't say a word at first. Back then it wasn't routine to have an MRI or CAT scan so there were no tools I could hold on to that could alleviate my fears. For the next four years I continually felt something suspicious with each self-breast exam. Knowing I had a second cancerous tumor hiding in my left breast that couldn't be felt made me crazy. What if the margins had been clear? If I hadn't needed a mastectomy it would have still been there, potentially growing without the doctor's knowledge. I continued to find lumps which needless to say led me back to the doctor. Finally, after the fourth serious scare, my doctor took pity on me and asked if I wanted to take care of the other side too. I was relieved to be asked, so I jumped at the option to have a second mastectomy and reconstruction. It wasn't a good time for another surgery, but is there ever a good time to have a mastectomy?

By this time I had divorced my husband, still working fulltime and raising my daughter myself. I had organized an 85 member Race for the Cure team at my office. I told my daughter that I wasn't able to do the race after all because of the upcoming surgery. She refused to hear such nonsense and said if necessary she would push me in a wheelchair. I had the second mastectomy five days before the race. Sure enough, a friend arranged for a wheelchair and my daughter and a couple of friends took turns pushing me along the race route. I was quite the sight. Since it was also my birthday, I had several dozen roses and balloons attached to my chair as we proudly participated in the 1997 Race for the Cure. Thankfully, when the pathology came back we got the great news that the right side was free of cancer.

I'm happy I made the decision to have the prophylactic mastectomy. Looking back, the surgeries and all the discomfort from a second mastectomy and reconstruction were well worth my long term peace of mind. I'm relieved that women now have that choice from the beginning. I remember feeling like a walking time bomb so, for me, being able to get a second mastectomy was the right choice.

From the time I went back to work eleven months after my diagnosis, I tried to put the cancer behind me and get on with life. I felt like I was the poster child for breast cancer. Since I was the first one in my circle of friends to be diagnosed with cancer I was pretty open about what I went through. People would share their personal stories or ones of their friends or family. My plastic surgeon called me frequently after I healed to ask if I would talk to one of his patients about having a mastectomy with reconstruction. I was happy to help and would call the nervous woman, arrange to meet for coffee or lunch and spend an hour or two talking about my experience. It was funny, we would talk all around the subject, and finally I would ask if she wanted to see how the reconstruction with implants actually looked?

Women were so cute! They would have never asked that of me, they were too embarrassed to request such a personal favor, but they were all very relieved to be able to see the final results. In one quick peek they could see the scars and the way the implants were positioned on my chest. This didn't change the fact they had cancer, but it helped reduce some of the worry of their own upcoming surgery. I could feel their anxiety simply drain away after seeing the appearance of my reconstruction. It was one less thing to be concerned about. As I reflect on those talks, I've recognized they helped me process my stuffed emotions as much as I helped them. I was able to process the buried emotions that earlier I hadn't or couldn't express easily. It was healing for me and in the process making me whole again. Knowing how it helped me, I often suggest something similar to other women who want to give back. Help someone else and you will inevitably help yourself. Who knew I was preparing for my true calling six years before the inception of Breast Friends? I guess God did.

Breast Friends

The work of Breast Friends actually started the day my friend Becky was diagnosed with breast cancer in 1996, three years after me. She was a more social person than me. I knew how lonely and depressed I felt throughout my treatment so I knew I needed to do something to ease that issue for her.

We worked together at a large corporation so I started doing little things, like keeping the 300 people in our department aware (with her permission of course) of what Becky was enduring. I would send weekly or bimonthly email updates with her address, telephone number, email address and what was going on in her world. She got lots of cards, telephone calls and visits from our co-workers which eased some of the time alone.

She and I were both working toward our bachelor's degrees when Becky was diagnosed. We were two weeks into our algebra class when she started chemo. Our professor was gracious enough to let me do homework with Becky so she could continue school without attending the class, which meant weekly visits from me to keep her up on the work. I would bring her a treat or a milkshake to brighten her spirits. She got through her nine months of chemo treatment while we finished two semesters of algebra in this way.

Fast forward to August 24, 2000, Becky called me to say she was going to the doctor. She had found another lump and was going to have it removed that afternoon. I insisted on going along just in case it was bad news. We sat together in the hospital lunchroom as we waited for her biopsy, trying to keep our minds active and not dwelling on the possible bad news. Over lunch that day we launched into one of those conversations about the deeper meaning of life, the kind of conversation that is designed to make sense out of crazy things that happen like cancer. We tried to find some reasonable explanation for why we both had been diagnosed with breast cancer, and why we both survived. We spent some time talking about the breast cancer environment and what seemed to be missing. She and I decided right there and then we had survived breast cancer for a reason. After much discussion we felt called to help women survive and thrive after a breast cancer diagnosis. Because of our experiences we understood how important emotional support and friendship was to the healing process. We didn't want other women to have to suffer with a breast cancer diagnosis alone because their loved ones didn't understand what to say or how to help them. We made a commitment over that lunch to help women survive the trauma of cancer…one friend at a time.

We didn't discover the meaning of life over that lunch but we did decide we would start a nonprofit organization. We decided on the name Breast Friends and after getting the great news that her scare was a false alarm we went back to our offices. Becky registered the name with the state and I registered the name for our soon-to-be website. It was a very exciting day. I remember calling Becky after I finished my task and asked, what's next? Neither one of us had any experience with nonprofit management so we didn't know how it would turn out. We agreed to meet every week so we could create a plan and keep each other moving forward. We may not have had experience but we had passion and talent and were willing to learn.

Since we were both taking college classes at Marylhurst University working toward our degrees, we found an intriguing weekend class we thought would give us the direction we needed. It was called, "Now is My Time," designed for women moving forward in their lifetime pursuits. We felt it would be a great opportunity to use Breast Friends as our class project and come up with a strategic plan to move Breast Friends off of the drawing board and into reality.

Why Am I Writing This Book?

A lot has happened at Breast Friends since 2000. We now have programs for patients from diagnosis, all the way through treatment, and for many years after. We offer emotional support to hundreds of women each year and provide helpful resources and information to their friends and families.

It became increasingly clear that medicine was doing a great job of curing breast cancer, or at least lengthening lives for these women, but their quality of life was still an issue. After completing months of intense treatment, surgeries and radiation, their lives had undergone a huge transformation and most women have a tough time getting back to their lives. These women have seen their mortality and now they are expected to pretend nothing has changed and jump back into life as it was before cancer.

In 2008 I became a Certified Life Coach so I had more tools to offer. I found women needed more specialized assistance at the end of their formal treatment. This is when these women have time to feel what they have endured. They asked complicated questions and wanted answers that were unique to each one. I found that the answers were in their hearts, they simply needed to be open to find them. This is when I created the Thriving Beyond Cancer workshop and retreat where women walk away after two full days feeling hopeful for the future and emotionally validated. This workshop provides the tools to help women find their unique path to the next chapter of their lives. The workshop has made a difference for so many women including myself.

This book is designed to validate your feelings and give you the same tools as the workshop I conduct. My dream of writing this book has become a reality. I talked about my dream during one of those retreats. One of my participants, Dr. Michelle Cameron offered to help me make my vision happen. I wrote this book to expand the reach of the Thriving Beyond Cancer message and offer it to each and every one of you, my readers.

This book will be one you can read over and over again, or you can reach into different sections as the topics become pertinent. We can't change everything in our life all at once, but we can work on change throughout our lifetime. This personal re-invention will allow you to change your thinking and make some changes now, and then more later if you choose. Change is an important component of staying relevant.

I love the term re-invention. I think of famous singers who had success in the past but need to reinvent themselves and come up with a new guise or a new sound that is more up with the times. Singers who successfully reinvent themselves have long, prosperous careers; those who do not are simply remembered for what they used to do. I, for one, want to continue to grow and change, even if at times it is uncomfortable.

I believe we all have something more to do on this earth, something great to offer to the world. The trick is to find out what that is and then to be brave enough to follow through with it.

<u>You are normal</u>. Most women who experience a cancer journey feel lost and alone after the treatments are finished. They need some direction, a road map, some guidance to find their best life moving forward. My hope with this book is to give you the tools you need to move forward. I would love to see you use the cancer journey as a springboard to the next and best chapter of your life.

Chapter 2

Let's Talk About the Cancer Journey

Many women say right from the beginning "Why Me?" I don't have a family history, as if that would make it okay or easier to deal with the diagnosis. The reality is most of the women diagnosed (85%) don't have a genetic connection. Having a family history isn't the biggest risk factor for getting breast cancer. Being a women and growing older are the two strongest risk factors for breast cancer. Even with a family history, I don't believe it makes the diagnosis any easier to accept or digest. Or patients say, I eat right and I exercise, so why did I get cancer? Unfortunately, those lifestyle choices are important to reduce your risk but there are no guarantees even if you are healthy.

So the question should be, why not me? The hard fact is one in eight women will get breast cancer in their lifetime. Actually, one in three women will get some kind of cancer in their lifetime. With the other risk factors like stress, obesity or being sedentary we are all subject to a diagnosis. The ones that really throw me are the young, fit and healthy women who were never sick before.

I remember attending my first survivor luncheon over 20 years ago. The keynote speaker was a beautiful young gal, in her early 30's. She was a runner with a lean yet muscular build. I remember thinking how healthy she appeared and wondered what her story had to do with cancer. She appeared to be the picture of health. She approached the podium and told her story while the audience was glued to every word. She had been diagnosed the year before with stage four breast cancer. The details are a bit fuzzy now but one thing I will never forget is the statement she made about her goals for the future. She said *"My goal is to run in every one of the Komen Race for the Cures in the US. There are 47 races, and my doctor says I have a 50% chance of living long enough to accomplish my goal."*

I couldn't believe what I had just heard. It hit me like a ton of bricks. How is it possible that a beautiful young athletic woman was fighting for her life and ultimately this disease would take her? From that moment on instead of wondering why me, I wondered, why did I live? Why was the cancer I had cured? And why would hers never be? I'm sure this experience set me up for what I was destined to do with Breast Friends. From that day I knew I had a higher purpose. I didn't know what I was put on this earth to do, but I knew I needed to do something to honor those who didn't have that opportunity. It didn't become clear until several years later when I sat with Becky over lunch waiting for her biopsy results.

When Am I a Survivor?

Being a survivor is a state of mind. When I was diagnosed with breast cancer, I opted to become a survivor immediately after that diagnosis. That was how I chose to deal with the unfamiliar and crazy space I found myself in after coming home from the doctor on that scary day. Obviously this is a personal journey and each of us needs to decide what survival means.

Since co-founding Breast Friends in 2000, we have had many women approach us and ask this same question, "When am I a survivor?" Is it after I'm diagnosed? Is it when I've finished all my treatment? Is it on my one year, three year or five year anniversary? I think we can all agree that it's a personal choice but in my opinion, if a person lives through the day of diagnosis, they are a survivor.

After hearing those fateful words, "you have cancer," it was as if my entire life flashed before my eyes. But not the life I had already lived, it was the life I was afraid I wouldn't see or be a part of in the future. For me, it was thinking about my youngest daughter who was only nine at the time. The thought of not seeing her and her siblings grow up, not seeing them finish high school or college, or not seeing them married with a family of their own was completely unthinkable. These are painful thoughts and thus far, well over 20 years since my diagnosis, I have been blessed to be able to enjoy those and many other important events in my life as well as in the lives of my children.

For me, surviving those private, scary moments and being able to pull myself out of the depths of my own private hell made me a stronger person — not just a survivor but a thriver! I made a conscious decision to go back to the doctor and fight this disease with all the strength I had. I chose to have all those surgeries and to put those poisonous chemicals into my system to kill any stray cancer cells that might be floating around. I chose to concentrate on living, not the alternative. I considered this journey a major inconvenience in my life and tried hard to find positive aspects in my life to help me get through. As a working mom I concentrated not on missing out on life but on feeling honored and blessed that I had more time to spend with my children.

Surviving and thriving during a cancer diagnosis and treatment is primarily mental. Don't get me wrong, cancer is an insidious opponent that not everyone beats, but while we are on this earth how we live and how we think make a huge difference in the quality of our lives. Cancer patients face many quality of life issues during their journey, including fear of recurrence, premature menopause, sexual and fertility difficulties, emotional distress, fatigue, lymphedema, cognitive problems and other treatment effects. Being positive during such a difficult time can be a tough proposition, but one I felt was worth the effort. I remember feeling so out of control at first, but by holding on to the concept of being a breast cancer survivor, I felt I was able to regain control.

The Ripple

I like to think of you, the woman healing from cancer, as the pebble thrown into the calm, still pond of life. The pebble creates rings that radiate from where the stone hits the water. The rings closest to the center are your closest connections, your children, parents, and other close family. For you, the patient, the emotional upheaval of waiting for test results, getting the diagnosis, the surgeries, the months of treatment, and then the recovery, all create stress and are traumatic. Your family and those closest to you are also traumatized and often completely thrown off balance. Chores, roles and responsibilities may have been divvied up and reassigned to make sure the necessities got done. Your sense of paralysis may have also affected those closest to you. The heart of the family has been compromised.

As in the pond, the ripples spread a long way from the center. The outer rings, people in our circles of influence who are not as close as our children, partner, siblings, or parents, also feel the disturbance. These might be friends, neighbors, church friends or co-workers. These people are certainly affected by the news but are less likely to be paralyzed with the fear that goes with a cancer diagnosis. Often these folks can spring into action and offer physical, emotional, social and spiritual support that will keep things running more smoothly. When you tell those outside your closest circle, they can often provide additional assistance your family may not be able to provide. They can run to the grocery store, do laundry, housecleaning or cooking. They can take the kids to soccer games or other activities; do things that free up the energy and time you need for healing right now. They can drive you to appointments or take care of you after surgery so your partner (if you have a partner) can continue to work so money continues to come in and the medical insurance stays intact. Delegating those small tasks may also allow you to keep working, if you desire.

People outside that inner circle can be less emotional; they may be great at taking notes at appointments, or being a sounding board for the tough topics. Having dialogue with other survivors can also be very helpful. Find someone who is far enough out from their own treatment so they can be objective and really listen to you and your situation. You will find that when you open up to others, people will come out of the woodwork. They may be your new best friend, or Breast Friend, as we refer to it.

Friends and other followers need to understand how to offer help in a way that will be accepted. As the patient, you need to embrace this help, give yourself permission to accept help when offered. Our tendency is to be flattered but say the standard thanks, I'm fine. Or, I will let you know if I need something, and then never let them know. Unfortunately, this doesn't help anyone involved.

Where Did Everybody Go?

Many women find themselves surrounded with loving friends and relatives for the time they are in active treatment and then, all of a sudden, treatment is over and so is all the attention, all the help, all the understanding. As soon as formal treatment ends or our hair grows back our loved ones assume we are good to go. They might continue to help with some of the physical chores you need done but you may need to find someone else to help with the emotional aspect. You may appear to be back to normal, but it will take some additional time to grow confident in your life after cancer, so take the additional assistance if it is offered or ask for it if it isn't.

Jan found *"the reaction from my siblings and mother were underwhelming. Because I didn't have to undergo chemo or radiation, my family assumed I was doing well. It wasn't until my mother was diagnosed with breast cancer and had a mastectomy shortly thereafter that she commented she had no idea what I went through. The emotional support I received from my husband, sons and friends was important to my recovery."*

Linda talks about her family. *"They were very responsive to me after the first surgery; my doctors both said I had to have someone with me for two weeks. After the second surgery, however, my friends and family were not as attentive and I was by myself for the most part. Luckily the limitations and discomfort was short-lived compared to the first surgery. But I did feel bad being alone. I knew they had their lives to live but I felt abandoned."*

Our Husbands and Partners Feel it Too

In most cases your partner loves you so much he or she would rather die than have you go through cancer treatment. This is how they are wired. They want to fix this, especially our men, but unfortunately this is something they can't fix. They hate to see you cry or feel bad about yourself. It's very painful for them to see you hurting, physically or emotionally, but they are in a Catch 22. If they say you are beautiful, we doubt their sincerity. How could they feel that way when you feel so ugly, scared or bald? But if they don't say those loving things we are convinced they don't love us anymore and are crushed. They really are in a no-win situation. This is where open communication can help. Say how you are feeling from your perspective, and then listen to what your partner is feeling. A cancer diagnosis can put tension on even the best relationships. Neither of you know what the other needs. You might feel numb, scared and angry throughout this unfamiliar time. A time when we need to arm ourselves with information and research so we can feel informed and empowered but at the same time it can all be so overwhelming.

Sadly, some couples will not survive a cancer battle. Everything that is already strand will have additional pressure. If communication is stressed, the cancer conversation could drive a bigger wedge of fear and vulnerability into the marriage. Fortunately, most couples will come out on the other side stronger and even more in love. Those relationships that have grown into a comfortable discomfort, that are a bit complacent, are the ones that are interesting to watch. We sometimes take our special person for granted, but the thought of that person not being there in the future brings us up short and reminds us of how important they are to us. These relationships find a renewed joy and zest for life that is wonderful to watch.

Some tasks and roles assumed by caregivers during treatment may need to continue while you re-immerse yourself into routines and slowly regain your energy. It's difficult to know immediately after treatment what side effects may be lingering and which will subside. Most breast cancer patients after their active treatment ends, find they need to continue with some sort of hormonal therapy which involves oral medications that are managed at home. These may take some getting used to physically and emotionally. Some are happy to take these pills feeling they are actively fighting the return of the cancer. These are topics that need to be discussed with your partner so they are on the same page with you and can relate to your feelings.

When you face a serious illness like cancer your partner or spouse has the most important role as caretaker of your soul. This role will go on long after the hair comes back and the scars start to fade. It's helpful for your partner to be there when you are finding your new place in the world after cancer. Roles may need to be redefined while searching for more meaning and depth in your life. This is a time when a woman re-evaluates everything from her marriage and relationships to her job or career to lesser things like her hobbies, friendships and the way she spends her time. Everything takes on a new light when filtered through the cancer lens. The pettiness of family squabbles or friends gossiping may encourage her to spend her time doing something she values more and feels is more worthy of her time. Not that she plans on dying any time soon, but since she has seen her mortality, she knows in her heart there are no guarantees of tomorrow.

We all cope with adversity differently. One sign of not coping with the issue or emotions may be denial. I believe denial has its place to protect us in the short term, until we can digest the full impact of a situation, but denial should not be a long term strategy. When we avoid any thoughts of the problem at all, or stay so busy we don't take the time or energy to deal with the problem, that isn't healthy. Of course it's easy to drown your feelings in drugs or alcohol but the issues don't disappear when you sober up and come to your senses.

Most women feel the need to re-align goals or start setting objectives that will feed their souls. Some women deal with depression or find it is exacerbated by the cancer. Confusion or depression can take root when feeling uneasy about our lives. We sometimes feel stuck without the tools to move forward. Partners can help you find your passion again. They can help you see things to be grateful for and help you focus on what you have rather than on what you have lost. Partners and husbands are invaluable in the recovery and re-discovering process.

My Friends and Family are <u>So</u> Done

Your family and friends are so relieved when you are finished with the formal part of your treatment and want you to get back to life as usual as fast as you can. Watching someone you love fight a disease like cancer is very painful. They want it done for themselves as much as for you. They have no control over the situation. They can't fix it. The vulnerability is excruciating and they can't wait for it to be over.

The problem is our family and friends think the cancer journey is finished with the end of the flurry of appointments. Like you, they don't understand or haven't been told it takes months for the chemicals to work their way out of your body. It takes time to recover from surgical procedures and other treatments like radiation. And even after the chemicals are gone and the areas heal, side effects of those treatments may linger.

Everyone is anxious to get back to their lives. As soon as the appointments stop, many of them disappear thinking you are finished. They assume, often incorrectly, that you are willing and able to pop right back into your old life. They don't know, and sometimes don't want to know, how difficult this may be. They have put their lives on hold too and are looking forward to getting back to normal almost as much as you are. The difference is, they can. They can walk away and get busy with their own lives, feeling good about how they stepped up to the plate and helped you out. Don't get me wrong, they should feel good. Many were selfless and inconvenienced their lives and the lives of their families to help you, but life goes on and they have done their part. Your challenge now is to complete your recovery emotionally and physically and keep on receiving the support you need to do so.

Leslie remembers, *"My family was excited for me to complete my treatment and anxious for me to start feeling better, but sometimes they forget that I'm not 'back to normal' and will never be the same person I was before."*

Deana explained it this way, *"It's like going through puberty all over again. Maybe it's puberty backward. Your hormones are changing, your body parts are changing, and your self-image is impacted in a big way, it goes on and on. I remember wanting my outside to look like my inside felt."*

Our feelings need to be validated during this time of uncertainty. No one, not even another survivor, knows exactly what you are enduring. We are all different.

Most of us don't do the emotional work necessary to process a cancer experience until it's over. Some women grieve immediately and all the way through their experience. Others may simply add all the appointments to their busy to do list and grieve when everything is finished. Another survivor certainly has an idea of some of the emotions, some of the turmoil a cancer diagnosis can create, but no one knows exactly what you are enduring. It is important for you to share those feeling with others, to get the assistance you need, so those near and dear have a sense of the journey you are facing. We all need people who are willing to understand, accept, and validate our feelings. Open up so they can try to understand. The people we spend time with, whether family or friends, may need to meet new criteria for friendship. Some of our friends may be downers, less positive and harder to be around. Those friends may not make the cut if they don't step up and change along with us. It's all part of the cancer experience.

Again, because our friends and family haven't been through the cancer first hand, they may not quite get it. They want to understand, but until they hear those words, "you have cancer," they just won't get it. They won't comprehend the lingering effects, the fatigue, or the sheer terror around cancer. I don't believe we simply get over it. I do believe however, we all have a choice to make about what we think about and what we say. Listen to your language. Focus your attention on your thoughts and how you express them. How do you talk about your life, the cancer, the future? If it is all negative, it may be time to rethink the message you are telling yourself and putting out into the world. Going through and getting beyond the cancer experience is a process, and for some it is a long bumpy road. However, that doesn't mean it's okay to dwell on the negative. You do have a choice, so make it a positive one.

But I'm Not Finished

Cancer changes who we are as individuals and it can be traumatic. It changes the outside, leaving our bodies scarred and different than before. It changes the inside as our body image is damaged, while our self-esteem and our self-confidence have been brutally attacked. No wonder we are an emotional wreck when our doctors congratulate us for being done and then move on to the next patient. I remember thinking, but I'm not done.

"My friends that haven't had breast cancer don't want to talk about it nor do they understand my stress or fears." Cory remembers. I have found it's up to us to communicate clearly what we are feeling and what we need from those closest to us. Sometimes that feels like an additional burden, especially for those of us who don't normally ask for help. I hear this over and over again with my ladies, "I've never had to ask for help," or "I don't know how to ask for help." Just like anything new, it takes practice. At first we feel vulnerable and that's uncomfortable, but think about it as a gift you are giving

your family and friends. Those close to you want to help but don't always know how. It's up to you to give them suggestions of what might be helpful. I have heard so many family members and friends tell me with tears in their eyes that they sincerely want to help but didn't want to be pushy, or call at the wrong time, or do something inappropriate. Teach them how to help you.

Educate your friends. Say something like "I'm so thankful for your call. Do you mind calling me back, I need a nap." Or "I'm at the doctors, I'll tell you when I'm finished and it's a better time to call." This direct approach works well with people. If your friend is especially sensitive she may be upset she interrupted or bothered you, she may feel embarrassed and not call back. This is how friendships can break down. Your friend may take your unavailability personally when it's really not about them. If you sense this has happened, do yourself and your friendship a favor, initiate the call back. Communicate your need for emotional, physical, social and spiritual support and how you see them helping in these roles.

As strong capable women, many of us lessen what we are experiencing. We minimize our feelings so others feel more comfortable. We are scared and miserable and we pretend we are fine. Then one day we can't be strong another minute and our network doesn't know what to think. If you find that you diminished what you went through its okay to have some conversation around how hard it was for you to be honest at that time. You were scared and didn't want to make others feel any worse than they did already.

Describe in detail that even though you are finished with the worst part of the treatment, you continue to deal with the fear, especially after receiving such intense care and now feel you are waiting for the cancer to return. Again, these fears may not be rational, but they are real. Remind them you are also dealing with issues the treatment has left you and how these side effects are affecting you mentally and physically. Consider this as an opportunity to teach those without first-hand experience what this crazy cancer world feels like.

Educate so that others can understand that although you have recovered physically, the emotional scars of treatment still need to heal. Clarify that, although the hair on your head is growing back, the effects of the chemo aren't. If you have chemo brain this doesn't go away as soon as the chemo ends, it can linger for months or even years, affecting your cognitive ability and, consequently, the way you feel about yourself. When I have trouble putting two sentences together in a meaningful way, it makes me feel crazy. Chemo brain can affect your ability to run the house, work, and juggle life the way you did before. Things that came easily before may take more concentration or work. This all affects our sense of worth.

When I was diagnosed I minimized what I was feeling and I didn't ask for help. I found myself feeling very alone. We need to ask for help. I learned this the hard way. Give yourself permission to ask for what you need, it will make the journey easier for you and for those around you. Then remember to tell those around you how important their assistance is to you. Say thank you and understand you will have your turn to help them at a later time.

Expectations and Fear of Disappointing Others

Many times we take on responsibilities for the family, the children, and the house, in addition to our own jobs, health and well-being. Some days I wonder who is taking care of me, but then I don't ask for help and wonder why I am overwhelmed. We all take on a lot whether we are in the middle of cancer treatment or not, and most of our responsibilities continue without much of a break. I remember thinking how I was letting others down when I couldn't do everything I wanted to get done. Honestly, twenty years out, not much has changed. As women we worry about what others think and hate to disappoint those who depend on us. I grew up with a specific idea of what a woman's role was in marriage. When I graduated from high school in 1971, Gloria Steinem was working hard to change the world and open up new options. The biggest problem with the women's liberation movement as I see it now is we took on a lot more responsibilities without a plan to take anything away. We ended up with pressure to do it all. Everything we did before the feminist movement and everything we wanted, including the career. This made for an overflowing plate all the time. Then throw cancer into the mix and all hell breaks loose. The guilt can be tough when we don't feel like we are meeting our own expectations, let alone our family's expectations. This is when you need to communicate how you are feeling and what you need so your friends and family can begin to understand. Even though you are finished with treatment, you aren't finished with the effects of cancer.

After the Breakdown of Expectations

Many women lament about relationships that didn't go well during treatment. The friends who didn't show up cause us grief and heartache leaving us feeling disappointed and sad. Feelings of bitterness and animosity bubble up. Where were they when I needed them? We feel anger, especially when that friend tries to walk back into our life like nothing ever happened. These friendships will never be the same without some serious conversations, and probably some tears and outpouring of emotion on both sides. Many relationships won't make it through this ordeal, especially if the parties involved aren't willing to be vulnerable and honest. It always makes me sad when someone allows a relationship to go off course because they aren't willing to put in the effort or deal with discomfort.

I believe people come into our lives for a reason. I think there are lessons to learn from all relationships no matter how brief or how painful. There are relationships that seem to blossom, even ones where we were barely acquaintances before a trauma like cancer. Relationships come out of the woodwork. Some people become our angels. They show up at precisely the right time and say all the right things. Some of these friendships will last for a lifetime. Some of our angels move on to help others in need and leave us with only the memory.

The friendships that tend to thrive are ones where there is open conversation, where feelings can be expressed, and even the scary emotions are shared. Some new budding friendships make it through this traumatic time, but some don't. The key is to be open to new relationships, be open to people helping you and your family. The phrase, "it takes a village" isn't an exaggeration. It takes many loving people to help keep our heads above water and to find our new life on the other side of cancer. If you are open to these new relationships, as well as to the more established ones, you will be stronger and more in touch with what's significant and valuable in your life.

When Our Friends Don't Understand

Our friendships can cover the huge distance between those very close relationships all the way to acquaintances. Some relationships will be stronger because of the cancer experience and others will fall away. Many women share their disappointment that some of their friends were so uncomfortable with the cancer, their baldness, or the possibility of them dying, that they completely fell off the grid. Then, when things were back to normal, they resurfaced and were surprised they didn't get a warm welcome. Friends often don't know what to say. Some handle crisis or tragedy with denial and put their heads in the sand and stay away for the duration of treatment.

To be fair, your illness may bring up in them a previous painful experience that hasn't been fully processed. The pain may be too great, and until you are back on your feet, they won't return or even explain their absence. When they do return they will act as if everything is fine between you and no time has passed at all. This is where open communication can potentially heal these wounds in both people. Both parties need to be compassionate to understand the others point of view.

Unfortunately, the damage is done. Sadly, without some damage control and good communication those relationships rarely survive. The patient feels abandoned and angry. The friend doesn't understand what they did wrong to cause those feelings. Perhaps you had this happen. What the best way to handle these situations? Do you forgive and allow them back into the inner circle or do you let them go? Either way, that relationship needs to be grieved right along with losing your breast, losing your youth or whatever other losses you have sustained through this journey.

Friends don't always understand what you are undergoing. In fact some feel very strongly they have been supportive through the treatment phase of the journey, but many a patient will disagree. I know I had expectations that were unrealistic. I thought my friends should know what I needed without my even telling them. I assumed people would call and check in on me. Unfortunately, some of my work friends were waiting for me to ask for help. I know now it was foolish of me to expect they knew what I was experiencing. They didn't. When I think back on it, when people asked how I was doing, I would answer with "I'm fine." Unfortunately, they took me at my word and thought I was fine, when I wasn't fine at all. Imagine that? So it's my responsibility to tell the truth and express my needs.

Friends and family need to understand how difficult this journey is, and without us minimizing it. They also need to understand how it feels to heal from a surgery or to be sick as a dog and unable to get out of bed after chemotherapy. You need to explain how bone tired fatigue makes you feel, like all the energy you have was spent getting up in the morning and doing a few family obligations. They need to understand the sadness, loneliness and depression that overwhelm and inhibit you from reaching out. Explain to them that you need to depend on them to make the effort and not wait for you to ask for help. They need to understand how difficult it is for you right now and continue to find ways they can contribute.

Sarah remembers how some of her friends were really there for her. *"You find out who your friends are! I don't remember telling some people about the cancer but somehow they knew. Old friends who used to be close became close again and visited with fleece blankets, frozen meals, treats, supplement drinks and an hour to talk. Neighbors who were considered acquaintances, became friends, shared their own stories of survival. They brought soup, books and leant an ear when somehow, from the distance across the street, they felt I might be having a difficult day. Family and friends, who are like family, becomes a daily reminder of who you really are and how well you are loved."*

Unfortunately there are those who can't deal with serious illness. Many survivors tell me that some of the people they expected to be there weren't and some they never dreamed to be there stepped up in a significant way. Most people want to be supportive, but their own fear is so great they can't seem to get past it to be there for you. This goes back to the fear of dying, fear of the disease, etc. Fears are not always rational, but they are real.

We all have friends who seem to flourish on drama. It might be their own drama, or it might be someone else's. Either way you can bet if there is no drama, they will create some. A friend who is no longer in the limelight because you have cancer, may not be able to handle the loss of attention since cancer trumps whatever crisis they can create. It might sound silly but I've experienced it myself.

Judy told me, *"I will never forget telling my best girlfriend about the cancer. I did not anticipate her reaction. She had a meltdown and had to talk to a counselor to help her deal with my diagnosis. She had lost a daughter to suicide a few years before. The possibility of losing her best friend was overwhelming to her. We are still close friends, but I really try to spare her the details of my latest medical challenge."*

Glenna talks about her friendships and what she has learned. *"Other friends let the cancer diagnosis become the key topic of conversation between us. I just want to be myself and talk about my art and other hobbies when we meet. Yet they could only evaluate the color in my face, how I looked, or how my energy was for the day. I have limited my contact with some friends due to their overzealous care.*

A couple of friends believe only in alternative cancer care and became critical of any traditional treatment choices I made. Both have strong personalities." Glenna continued, *"After a conversation where I felt I had to defend myself, I became emotionally and even physically drained. I limit what I share with them. It takes good boundaries on my part to keep their neediness from draining me emotionally and sap the energy I need to fight a life threatening disease. I am learning to balance my friendships."*

I'm Really Angry

Anger is a natural response to perceived threats. It's a warning bell that tells you when something is wrong. Anger causes your body to release adrenaline — the fight-or-flight hormone — which can increase muscle tension, heart rate and blood pressure. Anger might trigger or encompass other emotions, such as sadness, disappointment or frustration. Being angry isn't always a bad or negative emotion. It can help motivate you to change. It can allow you space to think about your relationships and create healthier boundaries. Anger becomes a problem only when you don't manage it in a healthy way.

When people get angry it usually stems from another emotion. If we feel embarrassed, threatened, guilty, vulnerable, or out of control, anger might be your first reaction. Anger might be a learned response to uncomfortable situations. Whatever the reason, it is a normal emotion that needs to be dealt with. When facing cancer we may feel fearful and out of control, so no wonder we get angry! Some find they are angry with themselves for ignoring symptoms, some are angry with their medical team for slow diagnosis. Sometimes we are angry at loved ones simply because they are there. We are all human and we all make mistakes. The trick is to deal with the anger in a healthy way so you don't damage yourself or others in the process.

When angry, you can choose to express or suppress the emotion. When we express anger we may convey it in a reasonable, rational discussion all the way to a violent outburst. When we suppress anger we attempt to hold it in or ignore it. This can include passive-aggressive responses in which anger isn't expressed constructively but instead in less healthy ways like retaliation or cynicism.

Since anger is a common emotion, ideally you'll choose constructive expression, stating your concerns and needs clearly and directly, without hurting others or trying to control them. When feeling out of control because of a health concern like cancer, it's easy to take out our frustration on those closest to us rather than dealing with the causes of that frustration. When you recognize these behaviors, stop and think about better ways to communicate your frustrations.

Some research suggests that inappropriately expressing anger, such as keeping anger pent up, seething with rage or having violent outbursts, can be harmful to your health thus counterproductive for a cancer patient or survivor. Such responses might aggravate chronic pain or lead to sleep difficulties or digestive problems. There's even some evidence that stress and hostility related to anger can lead to heart disease and heart attack.

Learn to control ones anger and express it in constructive ways can be a challenge for everyone at times. However, if there's a pattern of expressing anger in a destructive manner consider seeking help. If your anger seems out of control, causes you to act in ways you regret, hurts those around you, or is taking a toll on your personal relationships, professional guidance may be needed.

Glenna also talked about how she deals with anger. *"You do not travel down this road to recovery very far without potholes of anger. Anger is part of dealing with this disease. You may be angry that cancer has taken your career away or be angry at how others respond to you. You may be angry that you can't physically do what you want. I have often directed my anger toward my medical team. They are human and sometimes they screw up. Recently I had an infusion nurse flush a port with a drug that she knew I was allergic to. She was overworked and having a stressful day and just forgot.*

I use to get my anger out by digging in my garden. I do not mean casually tossing a little dirt. I would thrust the shovel deep into the dirt like I had to dig to China in an hour. However, a couple of years ago I tried that and set into motion lymphedema in my arm from overuse and repeated motions. Well, so much for that method. Someone suggested pounding a pillow, unfortunately any jarring motion sets off pain all around my port. Another suggestion was smashing ice cubes, or at least glaring at them until they melted!

Writing seems to help me. I write the uncensored version of how I am feeling and simply keep on writing over and over on the same page until no one can read it. At least I try to express my feelings"

What Do I Have Control Over?

The aftermath of a cancer diagnosis and treatment affects us physically, emotionally, mentally, spiritually and in more ways than we realize. The effects are there while we are undergoing our journey and for many years afterward. Many of us thought we had our lives under control, but cancer makes us reassess everything.

Control is an illusion. As much as we'd like to believe we have control over most things, our cancer has reminded us that we don't have control at all. The only exception is we do have control over our own behavior and what we think about, and even that can be tricky. Crisis and trauma give us the ability to find our real self. They can trigger our imagination and, if we funnel and direct that creativity and power we can design a new and more exciting life. If we cannot control our thoughts, we cannot control our lives. Practice methods to overcome your negative and scary thoughts and replace them with positive helpful thoughts that will move you toward the life you want to live. Many find yoga, meditation and other metaphysical practices helpful to quiet their minds, refocus concentration, reduce fear and gain a greater understanding of self and the world around them.

What do you want? What do you desire more than anything? That can be the secret to your ultimate success. Our subconscious mind doesn't discern between what we want and what we don't want. Our subconscious remembers and focuses on how we spend our time. Our mind is a powerful tool that can be used for good or taken for granted and wasted. The crisis and trauma around a cancer diagnosis can be used as a springboard to a more fulfilling life if you embrace the power you possess.

Don't Minimize Your Journey

Women have a tendency to minimize ourselves for the sake of others. We don't want others to be uncomfortable so we play down what we are facing. When asked how we're doing we say the normal, "fine" or "doing great, how about you?" Even if we feel like we are dying inside we can act as if nothing is wrong. Then, if we are fortunate enough to have found our cancer very early, maybe stage zero or one, or maybe it's DCIS or LCIS, what the doctors call precancerous or early stage, then we feel guilty for feeling bad. We finish our lumpectomy with radiation in record time and, instead of being proud of ourselves since we caught it early and acted accordingly, we minimize what we went through like we didn't suffer enough.

I talk about this a lot. The fact that you caught it early is a great thing, but it was nevertheless cancer. If you didn't have that mammogram or you didn't go to the doctor when you found the lump, it wouldn't have been so early or as easy. You have earned the label of survivor; wear it proudly. You had a lumpectomy or mastectomy, for heaven sakes. If you didn't have cancer you wouldn't have scars along your chest. So don't minimize what you went through for family and friends. Don't say, "I only had to..........." You had cancer. You were fortunate not to have to endure as much treatment as someone else but you went through most of the emotions any other person who's been diagnosed with cancer. Quit diminishing what you experienced, you had cancer. It was awful on many levels. This is part of your story. Own it, embrace it, and move past it.

You will endure many obstacles throughout your breast cancer journey. Each one is a step toward survival, growth, and moving you toward the new woman you are meant to be. The old you, may not survive this journey and for me that was okay. I found myself considering my life and saying, "If I can survive breast cancer, I can survive anything." I took the time to assess relationships in my life. The newer, more reflective survivor in me needed a reason to burst forth. I needed to be a survivor in more parts of my life than merely living through breast cancer. We all have 24 hours a day and we make decisions how to spend that time and who to spend it with. I don't want to float through life doing only what's expected of me. Rather, I try to make conscious decisions to improve my life and the lives of others every day.

Breast cancer was the catalyst for me to become a thriver. It was a blessing in disguise. It gave me a reason to really examine my life and make some changes about the person I wanted to be. I didn't know all those things at the time of my diagnosis and I'm continuously evolving even now, many years later. When I made the choice to be a survivor, I didn't understand the magnitude of that decision. But, making that decision has changed my life.

Survivor Guilt

Many women who are diagnosed at the same time as a friend and family member find themselves doing well with treatment while the other person does not. Unfortunately, cancer doesn't always behave the way we want or expect. I helped two ladies diagnosed with inflammatory breast cancer, one at 30 and one at 45. The 45 year old did not respond to any of the treatments and died within nine months of her original diagnosis. The 30 year old finished her treatments and is doing well several years later. Seemingly the same disease, the same doctor, the same treatment, yet why would treatment work for one and not the other? We don't know the answer to that question or many similar ones. We do know survivor guilt can cause depression, anger and much more, which can compromise your health. So talk about how you are feeling in a safe environment. You will find you are not alone and you can work through some of those feelings that tend to linger.

Quality of Life

Quality of life is a broad, multidimensional concept that considers a person's physical, emotional, social, psychological and spiritual well-being. These five areas affect the ability to perform normal daily activities. Emotional or psychological well-being helps maintain control over anxiety, depression, fear of cancer recurrence, and problems with memory and concentration. Social well-being primarily addresses relationships with family members and friends, including intimacy and sexuality.

Finally, spiritual well-being is derived from drawing meaning from the cancer experience, either in the context of religion or through maintaining hope and resilience in the face of uncertainty about one's future. Although quality of life may suffer considerably during and shortly after active cancer treatment, the majority of disease-free cancer survivors (five years or more) report a quality of life comparable to those with no history of cancer.

I've Finished Treatment, Now What?

Counting down the days or number of appointments on your calendar is not unusual when looking forward to the end of cancer treatment. Many women know exactly how many radiation days they have left, but when they leave the clinic for the last time, something happens. The woman, who was excited to never make that drive across town to see her radiologist again, finds herself feeling alone. She feels like a boat that has been set off to drift aimlessly in the sea. The moment your doctor says, "You're finished! I will see you in three months," the tidal wave of fear emerges. We have greatly anticipated those magic words, yet they seem to fall flat. They even provoke new fears, anxieties and concerns. It feels like the caring medical rug has been pulled out from under our feet.

Besides the initial diagnosis, this post active treatment period seems to be the most difficult to wrap our heads around. This is unknown territory almost like those days before the final diagnosis is delivered. Unfortunately, this timeframe is measured in months or years not a few days. Not even your doctor can reassure you about your chance of recurrence or how long it takes for the side effects to subside so you can feel like yourself again.

When the doctor looked me in the eye and said, "everything appears fine, no need to see you any longer," I remember walking away from that appointment confused. I had a sense that I could now finally get my life back, but at the same time, a terrible dread came over me. On one hand, while under the constant care of my doctor and their team, I felt I was actively fighting the cancer. Now being released back to my life I was conflicted. I knew it was positive to have the doctor confidently say I was cured, but it nevertheless gave me the weirdest feeling that it wasn't enough. How does he know for sure that the cancer is gone? Will the cancer come back? I understood intellectually that no one really knows the answers to those questions, not even the doctor. However, knowing these facts intellectually didn't give me the relief I needed.

I tried to assure myself that as long as the cancer was surgically removed, I was cured. The chemo and the Tamoxifen were for insurance, so I didn't need to worry, right? I wish it was that easy. Living through cancer changed me both inside and out. Obvious changes like the scars of the surgeries were more apparent, but the changes inside were more subtle but no less important. It seemed no one was talking about the emotional changes I had endured. Even more than 20 years later there isn't enough written about these changes, the whirlwind of emotions or what to do with those fears and other emotions once the treatment is behind you.

Am I Ever Going to Feel the Same?

My answer to you is no, you will never feel the same. You have faced your mortality. The reality is we all will die someday; the difference is those of us who have had the opportunity to experience life and death through the lens of cancer, know it. Things that were important may seem shallow or not worth our time any longer. With hindsight, I'm glad I had this awakening. It made me appreciate family, friends and experiences more than stuff. Don't get me wrong, I don't walk around in a dreamland, but I certainly appreciate what's important more than I did before experiencing cancer.

I spoke with a lady who wanted to keep her cancer a secret from her friends and co-workers. She said with complete sincerity, "I don't want cancer to define me." I gently told her it was certainly her decision to tell people or not, but cancer would change her life. I have spoken with thousands of women and that is a constant. Cancer doesn't have to define you, but it will have an impact on you.

Personally, I feel blessed I had cancer. I know that might sound silly to some but I feel that cancer has allowed me to find my purpose and live a life filled with helping others that is more rewarding than I thought possible.

Emotionally, I am different. I had a glimpse of my mortality; the possible end of my life seemed much sooner than I had ever imagined. I now understand the concept of death. Someday I will make that transition, and it could be from cancer. At 40 most of us don't even think of such things. I know I didn't until after I was diagnosed. I now know life is short and there are no guarantees of tomorrow. I was compelled to make a difference in my life and my community. One thing remains constant; cancer changes us, many in a deep way.

Whether you got the cancer-free nod from the doctor or you are managing the disease progressions, the only thing we all have control over is ourselves - our thoughts, actions, and reactions - nothing more, nothing less. Understanding this can help you relax and see the situation from a slightly different perspective. By reducing stress, eating healthy foods and working up a sweat by moving our bodies we can improve the quality of our lives. Even if we must live with cancer or the fear of it returning these simple suggestions will improve the quality of the life we have. We can make it through the treatments and go on to live a wonderful life, no matter how long or short it might be. None of us have an expiration date stamped on the bottom of our foot, so my wish for you is to live and enjoy the time you have right up to the end, no matter when that might be.

Chapter 3

What Happened to My Body?

In the next few chapters we'll talk about the physical and chemical changes many women experience after cancer and its treatment, the lingering side effects and how to cope with them. These changes, such as scars, fatigue, and menopause have emotional aspects that can affect our attitude, performance and how we experience normal daily activities.

No matter your choice of surgery for your situation, you are left with reminders. I try to see my scars as a badge of honor. These scars are on my chest because I fought hard to keep my life and endured several surgeries to remove the cancer and to reconstruct what once was a symbol of my femininity and womanhood. Whether the cancer left you with one or two breasts or none at all, we all have scars. These scars are emotional and physical. The most obvious of course are the physical and those are difficult at best to embrace each and every time you emerge from the shower and face the mirror. One of my ladies talked about having a single mastectomy and feeling disgust with her remaining breast. Her breasts that once represented her femininity and sexuality now sadly meant nothing but fat filled flesh.

Even when the doctor says we're cured, there's no magic wand they can wave to take away the scars and side effects. Because of the length of time it's been since my diagnosis I can give you a different perspective and new ways of thinking about your situation. You may need to use a "wait and see" approach to assess whether lingering side effects are temporary, or a permanent condition you must embrace. Everything we as cancer survivors experience is not okay. Some things, even after all these years, seem a bit barbaric. Nevertheless, there is comfort in knowing that you aren't the only one feeling like you do. Welcome to the sisterhood!

Why Did I Get Cancer?

If you feel betrayed by your body, you are not alone. I remember feeling like all the exercise and eating well completely backfired on me once I was diagnosed with cancer. I had lived by the motto of everything in moderation, I never smoked, and I didn't take drugs. When I drank it was always in moderation, in fact I was the designated driver for my friends since I was such a teetotaler. How did I get cancer? It didn't make sense.

No one knows for sure but most likely your body created a mutant cell and your system didn't destroy it, so it could multiply and take hold, becoming a cancer that needed to be dealt with. Linda laments, *"You look around at others living their lives and you wonder why do I have this disease? I might look normal but there's something alive in me that is growing and making choices for me. The funny thing is that you don't even feel like there's something there when you first get diagnosed."*

I remember thinking, how can this be, I feel fine. I didn't feel so fine after the treatment started or for a long time after it ended. Those affected by cancer used to talk about treatment like, if the cancer didn't kill you, the treatment would. Thankfully, it's much better than it used to be, with drugs to ease the nausea and other side effects, but don't kid yourself, it's tough. If you sailed right through treatment or were fortunate enough to have an easier time, consider yourself blessed, you missed that bullet. Most likely you caught another one or two along the way.

Leslie understands the complexity of all that we endure when she says, *"It was a relief to finish with my six major chemo treatments and get my appetite back and start to feel better, but I am still dealing with side effects. I'm experiencing mild neuropathy, edema, joint pain, and reflux; lingering fatigue, chemo brain and nail issues. I also have feelings of anxiety and the fear of recurrence."*

Some women will have ongoing side effects. Some will dissipate and others won't. Unfortunately, none of us knows for sure which is which. Ongoing effects aren't unusual. Hopefully they will get better, but if they don't, it helps for you to embrace them at some point and be able to move forward without resentment and anger.

Jan remembers, *"At the beginning of this process I truly felt my body had betrayed me. Then, I realized I am lucky to be living during this time. They found my cancer early and they knew how to fight it."*

Am I Ever Going to Feel Like Myself?

Many women ask me, will I ever feel like myself? The answer is yes and no. Cancer changes a lot about how we think and feel about things. It forces us to grow up and think about difficult topics most people avoid or think about when they are much older, but this is our lot in life. I chose to figure out why I didn't die, why I was spared and what I am supposed to do with this extra time I have on earth. I believe we all have a purpose in this life, but many of us don't know what it is until after a tragedy or disease like cancer hits us and we've had time to reflect on such things.

As time goes on your body will feel more normal. Most effects of the medications subside, or you get used to them. All in all, you start to feel more like your new self. Emotionally it takes a while longer to come to grips with what you have been through. I tease patients about how denial helps for a while but then the reality of what you have endured comes crashing down or sneaks up one day when you least expect it. The emotions can be overwhelming. Some seem fine through their entire ordeal, and all of a sudden the uncertainty and fear hits them like a sack of rocks.

A sweet woman called me one day and told me she finished her chemo almost six months before and all of her friends and family were amazed at how strong she was. She raised horses and she hardly missed a beat, continuing her duties around the barn, day in and day out throughout her treatment. Even on her chemo days, after a nap, she pulled herself together and got back to her routine. She told her friends and family she didn't want or need any help, she was fine. Six month after completing her treatment it hit her and she literally couldn't stop crying. By that time, everyone was busy living their own lives and now she couldn't get out of bed. We talked for a long time. I told her she was simply feeling the emotions of what she had endured during her diagnosis and treatment, and it was just a bit late coming. I suggested she contact her doctor and talk about some options. She may need a little helpful anti-depressant for a short time until she could work through these emotions and seek professional help to talk about all she'd experienced and was just now comprehending. This was a real eye opener for me as she woke up one day in crisis after dealing with her cancer seemingly well before that. We talked several more times and each time she felt better about things. It was important for her to grieve what she had survived, have her emotions validated and feel like she was normal.

Take Back Your Power

Taking ownership of your decisions will help you take back your power. Yvonne tells her story, *"The treatment for my cancer was incredibly challenging. But after six rounds of aggressive chemo and a double mastectomy, I heard the words, 'you're tests were negative...you're cancer free.' I thought, for a few brief seconds, that I was done. But within a few weeks I learned that it would be in my BEST interest to have radiation. Sometimes cancer treatment feels like one of those hamster wheels...you just keep running around and around in circles...hoping to get off, but not knowing when it's the right time to jump. I made the choice to stay on the 'wheel' and have the radiation. It was the best choice for me, because I would know that I had crossed my tees and dotted my ies. Yes, the treatment left me with other challenges to face. And over the years I've spent more time on that crazy wheel because of radiation issues. But I have chosen to own my decision and all of the side effects because I know I did everything I could do to save my life."*

A friend whose cancer came back in her bones told me, *"I caution women not to dwell on what stage of the cancer the doctor reports. I wish they did not connect staging and life expectancy, but they do. I personally think women would live longer if staging was removed from their vocabulary. I believe it can 'condition' women to die on schedule!"*

I know I had taken my good health for granted and, without good health, many other things didn't seem as sweet. So, for me, I figured out what is truly important. That included a closer look at my health. What am I eating? Am I getting enough exercise? Am I getting enough sleep? It's a lot more than merely these basic things, however. It's about how I spend my time? If my family is important, do I slow down long enough to spend quality time with them? If being connected to nature is important to me, do I spend time outdoors enjoying it? We will examine our values and what's important in more detail in chapter eight.

I Want My Body Back

If your appearance is important to you, and it is to most of us, then it is normal for you to initially be unhappy about what you see in the mirror after surviving cancer. It's part of this crazy path, and as difficult as it seems now, you can anticipate it will get better. We receive messages every day telling us what a woman's body is supposed to look like. Society and the media bombards us with unrealistic images and messages about how we should appear and how we should act.

Unfortunately, these ideals of body image don't start with normal women. And certainly don't take into account changes such as pregnancy, aging or enduring something traumatic like cancer. Even the supermodels displayed on the glossy magazine pages aren't good enough. Those photos are airbrushed, elongating that neck or slimming down those hips to meet some arbitrary and unattainable standard of beauty. Then, as busy career women and working moms, even before cancer we try to measure up to those unrealistic standards. Most of us have never looked like that, and if we did it wasn't for long and probably not recently. When I encounter a young woman who complains about her body, I gently suggest she appreciate that rockin' body of hers now. I usually get a funny expression and gently explain she won't always look as she does today. We laugh together but there is truth in my message. Life has a way of reminding us of our age and the differences from our youth.

With that being said, try not to compare your post treatment body with the faked bodies in the magazines, or even to the one you had last year. It can be hard on any woman's self-esteem. Figure out what "healthy" is for you now and strive for that. If you were in good physical shape before you were diagnosed and haven't been active during treatment, don't expect to walk back into the gym and start where you left off. It will take some time to build up your stamina and it might take longer than you hoped. We will never again have the body we had at 20, so practice self-compassion when you gaze in the mirror. In fact, practice self-compassion in all areas of your life. If those dishes are piled in the sink from dinner or you didn't complete today's to-do-list, it's okay. Be gentle on yourself as you start to get back on your feet and your energy returns.

If you had a lumpectomy and radiation, your breast is most likely a different shape or size than it once was. One breast is likely smaller or different than the other with a scar or two that reminds you every day of the ordeal you recently finished. One morning I helped fit a lady with a partial prosthetic. She came to me three years after her treatment ended. She didn't realize there was anything she could do to deal with the different sizes of her breasts. She had undergone a lumpectomy followed by radiation and found she had two radically different sized breasts. She tried stuffing the smaller side with socks or other material but soon gave up. Her solution was to go without a bra since she was impossible to fit. She came to a Breast Friends event and found that one of our programs provides free prosthesis to women without insurance and within a week of that event she made an appointment to come to the office. She told me she had not looked in a mirror for over three years. She lived alone so she hadn't shown her scars to anyone until that day. I felt honored that she allowed me to see her and help her in that very personal way. I was able to fit her with prosthesis to make her feel good about her image. I showed her a new silhouette in the mirror where both breasts appeared the same and it brought tears of joy to her eyes. Her mismatched breast now fit nicely in a bra that was the correct size for her remaining breast. The partial prosthesis filled in the previous gap making her feel whole for the first time in over three years. I love my job!

Another lady tried everything to get her cotton fluff prosthesis on her mastectomy side to stay in place. She was unaware of weighted prosthesis and pocketed bras, where the prosthesis fits snugly in the pocket staying in place. She told me, *"My bra would ride up on one side and I had to adjust it all the time. One day I got real creative when the frustration was too much. I found an old ironing board cover elastic clip and attached one side to my bra and the other side to my pants. It worked pretty well, but caused me problems when I had trouble getting it undone on one of my many urgent potty breaks."* We were able to fit her with the correct bra size and prosthesis to regain her confidence and get rid of the elastic clip she used to improvise.

Donna remembers how she had two choices, *"Mastectomy and reconstruction with no chemotherapy or radiation, or lumpectomy with radiation. I felt like I had to make one of two terrible choices; I hated all the choices and the fact that I had cancer."*

Survivors talk about how difficult it is to see the surgery site after the bandages come off. It's not merely at the beginning, even though that may be the hardest time. These scars are a constant reminder of the trauma your body and soul has lived through. For those who had radiation, even the tiny dots tattooed designed to direct the lifesaving radiation beam remind us of those days we went back and forth daily to the clinic for treatment.

Kathlene lamented about the night before her lumpectomy surgery, *"What if they find the cancer is worse than they thought and decide to remove my breast?"* She remembers caressing her breast, really feeling her breast and the grief associated with its potential loss.

Another survivor shared that *"The mastectomy scars were the bad ones for me. I didn't even look at them for the first 3 weeks. When I finally had the courage to face myself in the mirror, I didn't expect to see divots on my chest. The indents and the loose skin were horrific. It wasn't until I had the expanders put in months later that I began to feel some sense of normalcy. At least they filled in the indents."*

Another survivor explained how losing the breast was difficult but she wasn't prepared for the shoulder pain, chest stiffness and loss of movement, sending her to frequent physical therapy.

Reconstruction is getting better all the time, but your new breasts will never be the same as the originals. I had implants for many years and I lovingly called them placeholders. After a few years they were hard and uncomfortable. The little round hockey pucks disguised as breasts appeared adequate in clothes so they did their job of filling the space designed for breasts. Plastic surgeons are perfecting several other procedures using your own body fat to reconstruct breasts alone and with implants to reduce the hardness that sometimes results from scar tissue strangling the implant. One of these newer reconstructive surgeries is the DIEP (Deep Inferior Epigastric Perforator) flap procedure where belly fat and skin, but not muscle, is micro surgically removed and placed in the breast area, connecting it to a blood supply. It's a tough 11 to 12 hour surgery but can have amazing results. I have to admit, they bounce like real breasts and those who've had the procedure even have cleavage again.

If you are fortunate enough to have had nipple sparing surgery, even though the nipples don't work as they once did, it is nevertheless wonderful to still have them. If you haven't had surgery yet, I suggest you ask your doctor if that is an option for you. If the doctor feels it is too risky, and depending on the nature of your particular situation, then you can always consider nipple reconstruction or tattoos when the reconstruction is finished. Many women feel that having some type of nipple or tattoo takes the eye off of the scars left behind from surgery and gives a more pleasing, more natural appearance. It's an optical illusion caused by drawing the eyes away from the scars and concentrating them on the nipple area. Fortunately the redness of the scaring will also fade with time, making the scars much less noticeable.

Tattooing is also a great way to deal with lingering scars, with or without reconstruction. Some women and their partners find it sexy to cover the entire areas with vines, flowers or even lacey tattoos. One woman told me she wanted to use white ink and have a feminine lacy camisole drawn on her mastectomy scars. I didn't actually see it but it sounded beautiful; I'm considering it myself.

The desire to be whole again is one many women struggle with. No matter how many surgeries, no matter how wonderful your plastic surgeon, you will have scars and your reconstructed breasts will never be like the breasts you lost.

I was pretty small chested so having a mastectomy made sense when I didn't have clean margins, but even so it didn't make the decision any easier. Thank goodness it isn't like it was when my aunt was diagnosed in the sixties. She went into surgery not knowing if she even had cancer. She went in whole and didn't know if she would come out with her breast or not. While under anesthesia the pathology of the lump was assessed. If the lump was benign the surgeon tidied up the area and sewed you back up. The patient woke with a small incision and went on with her life. If it was malignant she woke up several hours later after a complete radical mastectomy, removing not just the breast tissue but also the underlying muscle and all the axillary lymph nodes. That's what happened to my aunt. She woke up from that deep sleep to the reality she had cancer and no breast. I can't imagine how the doctors made such a life altering decision while women were under anesthesia. I was a child when she endured this barbaric procedure so I didn't understand what she went through until many years later. Thank goodness there have been dramatic improvements to the way cancer is diagnosed and treated. At least now we have time to process the fact that we have cancer, understand and choose our surgical options and see examples of what we might face when the surgeon is finished.

For many years, reconstruction wasn't available and women had to contend with primitive prosthetics or stuffing socks in their bras. Now, in the US, the Federal legislation mandates that all insurance carriers give women the option of reconstruction. We have the right to undergo reconstruction to create a more natural breast to replace the one or ones that were surgically removed and reduce, lift, or enlarge the other to match.

Sadly, some women have medical conditions that prohibit reconstruction. Glenna's doctor had to say no to reconstruction after a heart issue posed too big a risk for her to undergo such a major surgery. Many women, who have radiation and even with new technology, must wait a year or two before attempting reconstruction for the best results.

I felt fortunate to move through my reconstruction process more quickly since I didn't need radiation. Funny thing was, I thought by getting through the final surgery more quickly I could move on with my life. I felt that when my final surgery was behind me, I would be done; like I could simply flip a switch in my brain and I would no longer think about cancer. I certainly wanted cancer behind me, but I soon understood that would not be the case. My body may have healed, but there was a lot more healing that needed to happen. The emotional scars were a lot deeper than the ones on my chest and much more difficult to heal. I have devoted later chapters to healing the emotional scars. Until then, let's move on and talk more about other physical side effects that you might be experiencing.

My Hair is So Different

Our hair is a very important part of our identity and our self-image, so losing it can be liberating or devastating. There's no way to sugar coat it. It's a real bummer to lose your hair due to chemo. It's more than the hair itself, it's truly about what it represents. Hair loss screams "cancer." Our surgical sites can be hidden by clothes, camouflaged so that no one needs to know we had surgery unless we want them to know. When a woman has her surgery to remove the cancer, those scars, even a complete mastectomy with no reconstruction, can be covered with a larger shirt and extra layers, but when you lose your hair, the whole world knows. It's like a coming out party for you and the cancer, but no one is in the mood for the party.

Kathlene shared her experience. *"A woman walked up and tried politely to ask if I had cancer. At first I was angry, it felt like an intrusion. But then I thought she might be facing the same thing and was just trying to connect. We talked and she was going through cancer just like me."*

It's up to you whether you want to talk about the cancer with others. When our beautiful locks start to shed, the bald head, whether covered by a hat, scarf or a wig makes the statement to the whole world, *'You've got Cancer.'* My good friend Becky remembers when she went to a restaurant shortly after her hair fell out. She was searching for a table and passed by two ladies already seated eating their lunch. They stopped everything and said with that look of pity, *'That poor thing, I bet she's got cancer."* None of us want to be *"that poor thing."* For those experiencing baldness it can be a turning point. Many make the decision not to go out in public or at least limit their time out in the world, others rock their bald head like a badge of courage. Either way, it's a highly visible and tough part of the journey that can stay with us for a very long time.

Marianne recounts, *"By the second round of chemo I was losing my hair. There is nothing that prepares you for this. I had shoulder length hair and when it started falling out it was everywhere. I couldn't go anywhere without leaving a trail. My pillow would be covered! After dealing with that for around 10 days I had my husband shave it off."*

Losing your hair can feel like losing your identity. Women spend billions of dollars every year getting their hair done: cutting it, curling it, straightening it, dying it, using products to make it thinner or thicker. So losing our hair feels like losing a piece of ourselves. I remember a woman I met right after she was diagnosed. She told me flat out she wasn't going to do anything about her cancer because she wasn't willing to lose a breast or her hair. She was from a wealthy family and her image was everything. In truth, she couldn't deal with the shame of losing either one. Unfortunately, I wasn't able to change her mind and instead she started drinking heavily to cover her pain. After a year and a half she woke up one day, contacted her doctor to have the surgery, and started chemo. Unfortunately by then her cancer had metastasized and she only lived a few more months, bald and without one of her breasts. How sad.

This is an extreme example, I know. So much of this woman's self-confidence depended on her appearance. She didn't know who she was without her hair or her breasts. After I met this woman and better understood her story, I appreciated how brave the rest of us are to start and finish cancer treatment, to face the scars, hair loss, and the unknown effects of treatment. We are the brave ones, so congratulations for having the courage to treat the cancer. You have gone to each and every one of those appointments, and found a way to move forward. The aftermath of cancer is uncertain. Embrace the decisions you have made and the heroic efforts you have endured.

Darcy was told by a co-worker who had her own battle with cancer about her hair loss. *"I lost hair in places I didn't think of. I was talking to a co-worker who told me of her continual runny nose and occasional nose bleeds. She said you know you don't have any nose hair to capture and filter stuff anymore. I stood there in shock and said, 'how could I not know this'? Sure enough I went to the bathroom and looked in my nose and I had no nose hairs."*

Janice remembers how she was told her hair would fall out within 15 days of her first chemo. *"Sure enough it started coming out in handfuls, so I had my son help me shave off the remaining hair. It was more upsetting to wake up in the morning and have my pillow look like the cat slept there. I remember one day I looked in the mirror and most of my eyelashes were gone, eyebrows too. Luckily a week or so later I noticed a bunch of baby eyelashes growing in between the few I had left. A few days later those remaining lashes were gone but I had the new ones growing in strong."*

Sarah remembers her hair loss. *"I never thought too much about my hair until I didn't have any. Wearing a hat to work the first day was the hardest but, once I was there and out with the co-workers, it was fine. It was winter, so it was a good time to cover my head. When the hair started to come back, I was reluctant to show the new growth. The radiology nurse said, "It is your hair and you should own it." It was difficult again to go to work and show my new, gray, half inch of hair. Again, after I arrived, I was fine. I was actually proud. I had been through a war and I had won! Months later my new, curly, very gray hair was a constant reminder of the battle. The day I decided to get it colored was a relief. I looked in the mirror at the salon and saw the 'me' before the BIG C. It brought tears to my eyes. I was back!"*

Ways to embrace the hair loss may be things like dying it a funky color, especially when it's going to be gone in a week anyway. I have seen photos of women who tried the Mohawk style. It's not something I would do for a long term hair style choice but it can be fun for a few days. Color the tips or try a new asymmetrical style where one side is short and the other longer. Shave only underneath or shave it off completely and have a henna tattoo (temporary) of your favorite design on your bald head. Fortunately, in most cases, hair comes back after losing it from chemotherapy. You may notice it has a different texture, different color, or may even be curly if it was straight, or vice versa, but it usually comes back and eventually goes back to the way it used to be. These changes are normal and can have a component of fun. My hair came in very white in the front and then salt and pepper in the back. I enjoyed soft curls at first, although they eventually straightened out after about a year. I have seen some people's hair come back curly as a poodle. Some women's hair comes back rather straight, but almost always it is different than what it was before chemo.

I love it when a woman comes in with a short sassy hairdo she has kept well after her chemo grow-out, a hairstyle she would never have considered before being bald, and she completely rocks it! Many women would never have cut their hair so short or experimented with it like this under normal circumstances. Hair is an extension of our personality and you might find you love the new look and so does everyone else.

Either way, have fun with it, experiment with new styles and colors. I spoke with a 30 year old who had the most gorgeous long dark brown hair and after the first chemo it all started coming out. She took our advice and had some fun with it. She decided to have a hat shower where friends and relatives all brought her a fun, funky or practical hats. She bought a cute wig and shaved her head during the party so she felt like she had control over something in her life. Her friends were there to boost her with laughter and tears. They took photos and the party has been a cherished memory since. She did her research and decided to donate her hair to [1]Locks of Love, a public non-profit organization that provides hairpieces to financially disadvantaged children. These kids under age 21 are suffering from long-term medical hair loss from any diagnosis. She felt great knowing her hair could go to someone else who needed it. When her hair grew back she was thrilled. For the very first time in her life she had curly hair, and as it grew out longer and longer she carefully did everything in her power to keep her ringlets. She was disappointed when I told her it would most likely go back to her pre-cancer straight hair, but for about two years she enjoyed those curls.

One way to remember this time in your life is to capture it on film. At Breast Friends we partner with a photographer and a makeup artist to celebrate the baldness stage. We invite our ladies who have lost their hair from chemo to allow us to capture it on film. Our Bald is Beautiful program is quite a hit and those photos are a wonderful reminder of how brave they were during this portion of the journey. We display these images proudly in the office for all to see.

Help, My Arm is Swelling!

Lymphedema is a build-up of lymphatic fluid which causes swelling. Any woman who has had some of her axillary lymph nodes removed or who has had radiation therapy is at some risk for lymphedema. The risk increases as more lymph nodes are removed. Between eight and 56 percent of women develop lymphedema after breast cancer surgery.

---

[1] Locks of Love: wwwlocksoflove.org

Lymphedema can occur days, weeks, months, or even years, after surgery. 80 percent of those who develop lymphedema do so within three years of surgery. However, with proper precautions, lymphedema can be avoided in most women. With the advent of sentinel node dissection fewer women develop lymphedema, but even that doesn't ensure you won't have issues with this common side effect. For those who do face this condition, it can be serious and very uncomfortable.

I'm fortunate to have had only a very mild case of lymphedema despite having ten lymph nodes removed. Some women aren't so lucky and have swollen limbs every day. The compression garments help but they aren't exactly stylish. I have seen some that appear like a sleeve of tattoos with colorful patterns but that's not for everyone. The compression garment helps contain the swelling but can be uncomfortable, especially in hot weather. Be sure to consult your doctor for the location of a certified fitter, so you can be properly measured if you are experiencing swelling. The fitter can assess what compression garment would be best for your situation.

A woman that attends one of our support gatherings told me her story of developing lymphedema after trimming her rose bushes. She poked herself on a thorn through her gardening gloves. Her surgeon had done a routine sentinel node dissection removing only three nodes with her mastectomy. It seemed innocent enough but within a couple of weeks of her rose thorn poke she was in serious pain, on antibiotics, and she's been dealing with lymphedema ever since.

A similar complication includes a condition called cellulitis. It is a bacterial infection of the skin that is characterized by swelling, redness, tenderness and heat in the affected area. According to Mayo Clinic it can spread rapidly to the lymph nodes or bloodstream, causing life-threatening consequences. Yvonne found herself dealing with this unexpected issue and found within a few days had gotten pretty serious. Her arm had gotten very hot, red and swollen within a day or so and just overnight had doubled in the area covered. She was treated with antibiotics and hasn't experienced further complications.

Some survivors find massage and/or acupuncture helpful in dealing with the swelling and discomfort of lymphedema. Some physical, occupational, and massage therapists are specially trained to perform lymphatic drainage. They can also teach you how to do the massage techniques yourself between sessions to relieve the discomfort. Talk to your insurance company and see what benefits you have to help with the expense. If insurance is an issue, ask the therapist if low cost or sliding scale options are available. It's worth the time and trouble to locate additional resources in your community and talk to others who have gone before you.

One lymphedema specialist said *"lack of knowledge can cause unnecessary anxiety and fear. Inaccurate information can have life-changing consequences."* She hears things like, *'I was told I can't go running ever again. I'm really upset because I love to run. I'm getting fat and so is my dog.'* Or *'I know I can't ever go on a plane again, and I had my heart set on a trip to Paris.'* Happily, these things are **not true,** but talking with a specialist is appropriate to make sure you have accurate information for the prevention, early detection, and management of lymphedema.

Paula found her problems started after radiation. *"After having my arms over my head for 20 minutes at a time without moving, five days in a row for six weeks I noticed some stiffness in my left shoulder. After months of aggravation and increasingly limited mobility, I got some physical therapy. The greatest most helpful information I received was how to do lymph drainage massage on myself and why it is so important to keep my arms moving. So now*

I do lymph drainage every day, it only takes a couple of minutes and helps keep my shoulder limber and reduces any pain I may have in my breast."

Many women feel embarrassed to sport the lymphedema sleeve. They are troubled by the fact they can't wear certain clothing because of the swelling in their arm. I don't blame them, but just like scars, try to imagine these sleeves as badges of courage. Sometimes a change in the way we think about something helps in the healing. If the condition persists even with therapy find ways to accept or at least manage the condition. Perhaps use the sleeve as an opportunity to educate others about the condition and bring more awareness to your community. Like many of the aspects around cancer, things are improving so don't lose hope.

I'm So Tired

Fatigue is one the most common issues from both chemo and radiation. We all get fatigued from a busy week at work or lots of activities with the kids. But this is the bone tired kind of fatigue, the kind a nap doesn't help all that much. There isn't much you can do about this exhaustion other than rest. Your body is in overdrive repairing the damage the chemotherapy and/or radiation has done. The part that is difficult to understand is how long it actually takes our bodies to heal. Fatigue starts from the very first treatment and continues for weeks or months after the treatment has ended. When chemo is working properly, it is killing <u>all</u> the fast growing cells in your body. That's why some chemo patients have some tummy upset. There are millions of fast growing cells in our digestive system. Thank goodness for anti-nausea drugs to help combat most of that. But the constant repairing leaves us drained and stripped of our reserves, creating extreme exhaustion. Even all of the surgeries that either precede or finish up the process take their toll. Also, don't forget the effects of anesthesia on your body. In my case I had six surgeries in 11 months, all requiring full anesthesia.

Some people sail through chemo and find the radiation kicks their butt. Some find they make it through the formal treatment and when they attempt to resume normal daily activities, they are so overwhelmed and exhausted they need the security of their afternoon naps. Published reports on the prevalence of cancer-related fatigue in survivors vary widely; however, studies suggest that 17-26% of cancer survivors' deal with persistent fatigue months to years later.

Sick and Tired of Being Sick and Tired

Some women experience problems long after treatment has ended, some may be minor but some may impose terrible physical challenges. It's important to talk to your doctor about the effects of each therapy and what might minimize their effect on your quality of life. It's okay to question your doctor if you experience severe side effects. Understand that your doctor is working for you. Our medical teams are well versed in the disease, the treatments and all the statistics from studies, but everyone is unique and can react to drugs differently. Having a conversation will make sure your treatment options are giving you the best quality of life possible.

Will I Ever Get My Energy Back?

Yes, you will eventually feel more like your old self, but give yourself time. The cancer was the enemy and the artillery was the surgery, chemotherapy and/or the radiation. Your body has been ravaged by the effects of the war and it will take time and patience to feel like your old self again.

The prescribed anti-hormone drugs take some acclimating. These drugs can keep our bodies in a state of flux, slowing down the process of getting back to normal. If you feel like you can't get out of bed, or the energy isn't returning like you think it should, talk with your doctor. Depression can manifest itself in several ways, including physically, so be aware that if energy continues to be low for too long there may be an emotional component that also needs to be addressed.

We need to allow our bodies the time and the fuel they need to repair themselves. Whether you are in treatment or you're finished, you will have your good days and your bad ones. One day you might feel great, and then you might find yourself on the couch for the next few after overdoing it on the days you felt better. Most survivors will tell you it took much longer than they thought to get back to normal daily activity levels, so be kind and gentle on yourself.

Make the best of the good days; take advantage of the energy and stamina you have. Plan something fun, live your life. Plan it and, if necessary, cancel if you are too tired. Understand that you may not be able to do everything you want to do. It takes time to recover, so give yourself permission to lay low for a while. If you go back to work part or full time after being off, it will take some time to build up your stamina there as well. You may be able to work, but nothing more. Discuss your options during this time with your employer so they understand your needs. Regulate your activity level depending on how you are feeling. Your main job now is to get your health back. Take control over your health by eating well, exercise, and get plenty of rest.

During this time it can be tricky to juggle your time, but try to stay connected with people as well. It can be easy to isolate yourself so make it a goal to pick up the phone and call at least one person per day so you can keep relationships intact. Try to explain to those who matter how odd this time feels and that it will take some time and effort to get back to your old activity levels.

When friends call to get together, one woman tells her friends, *"I'm sorry but this is a one event day. An event is usually going somewhere like the doctor or grocery shopping. I seem to move between one and three event days. I've used my event up for today."* They won't know or understand unless you have this conversation with them. They need to comprehend how you are feeling in order to help you through this time. It's an effective tool when you are trying to explain how you feel to family and friends when your energy and stamina haven't yet returned. When our hair is back, the world thinks we're back; we're all done with treatment and so everything is should be fine. They assume we can do all our chores, and some of theirs too since we've had this nice little break.

Radiation can sometimes throw people into a false sense of security since it is over so quickly each day. Nonetheless, the accumulation of your sessions, day after day, for six or seven weeks can take its toll on the skin and your energy reserve. I know a woman who got through the entire six weeks of radiation treatment unscathed but as soon as the radiation was over, her skin broke down and so did she. She wept for two weeks. Unfortunately, there is no timetable for the recovery. Each person is as different as the cancer, and so is the recovery time.

When I went through cancer treatment it seemed like the world was going on without me and that truly bothered me. It's like the whole world is on this merry-go-round and getting cancer was like getting kicked off the ride. The bumps and bruises I felt as I picked myself up mended, but the isolation I felt hurt deeply. I hated the thought of missing out; missing all that was going on. Knowing what I now know, I understand that the fatigue takes time to subside because of the amount of repair my body was undergoing and we don't have the ability to maintain the same level of activity as we had before cancer. We can resume previous activity levels eventually, but not immediately. It's important to understand you will get your energy back again but it takes time and patience.

Who Sleeps?

Many women complain of sleeping problems during and even after cancer treatment. Poor sleep reduces overall quality of life. Sleep is essential for our bodies to heal from surgeries, chemotherapy and radiation. It's also needed to optimize immune function and our overall mental health. Medical evidence suggests that for optimum health and function, the average adult should get seven to nine hours of sleep daily and may need more when recovering from cancer.

Up to 80 percent of cancer patients suffer from insomnia. In addition, symptoms of insomnia were found in 23 to 44 percent of patients two to five years after treatment for cancer.[2] These are alarming numbers. The psychological trauma of cancer can cause patients to lose sleep. I'm sure we've all had times in the middle of the night where sleep eluded us because of worry and anxiety. Pain and other symptoms from the cancer itself and adverse effects of treatment, such as nausea or hot flashes, can interfere with sleep. Most women experience sleep issues to some degree, whether it's worry, menopause, or medication side effects. Whatever the root causes, if you aren't getting good sleep, the time it takes for your body to repair will be longer.

---

[2] https://www.oncolink.org/support/side-effects/insomnia/sleep-problems-insomnia-in-the-cancer-patient

When dealing with long term sleep issues consult your primary doctor, oncologist and/or a specialist. Make sure your doctors are communicating with each other so they can agree on your treatment. One patient took six different medications, including some habit- forming ones for her sleep issues. When her oncologist found out, he immediately removed her from all her sleep meds and suggested some different options that lessened her sleepless nights and reduced the number of drugs she used. Insomnia can lead to fatigue, memory and concentration problems, mood disturbances and psychiatric disorders. Studies suggest that insomnia may play a role in physical symptoms, shorter lifespan and immunosuppression. For these reasons, and to improve quality of life, patients should seek and be offered treatment for insomnia.

It's Either Numb or It Aches

Chemotherapy drugs, especially Vincristine and the Taxanes, can damage sensory nerve cells, causing painful sensations in the hands and feet (peripheral neuropathy) and result in chronic pain. Patients often complain of skin sensitivity when they attempt to bear weight on their feet. Some experience problems standing for long periods of time, walking long distances and have balance difficulties. They may have increased risk of falling, sensitivity to heat or cold, and numbness with tingling or pain.

My friend Becky can't sleep with her covers tucked in over her feet, that extra pressure on the tops of her feet increases her pain to an uncomfortable level preventing sleep. Another friend has to be extra careful walking especially on stairs as she can't feel the bottoms of her feet. The extent of the damage is directly related to the dose of the drug and can take months or years to resolve, if ever.

Some patients taking Xeloda and other drugs are affected by Hand-Foot syndrome, which is a tender redness that resembles sunburn on the palms of the hands and soles of the feet. The affected areas can become dry and peel, with numbness or tingling. Hand-Foot syndrome can be uncomfortable and can interfere with the ability to carry out normal activities. Deborah remembers, *"I took Xeloda for 6 months. It didn't make my hair fall out again but it caused hand and foot syndrome which made me unable to button my shirts and unable to wear regular shoes. I wore slippers to work and had my husband help me get dressed in the morning,"*

There's a therapy used with diabetics to increase blood flow and reduce the discomfort from neuropathy now being used for effects of chemotherapies. This and other improvements to combat the latent effects are emerging every day, so talk to your doctor about these issues so you know about all the newest remedies available.

Some cancer survivors also experience pain associated with their surgery and radiation, even when they are cancer-free. Suzi talks freely about the sensation she has in her breast years after her lumpectomy and radiation. *"It feels like there's a party going on in there, the nerve endings are coming alive, still repairing themselves. It is the weirdest pain and twinges; it feels like an electrical current."* The degree of pain depends largely on the type, location, and stage of the cancer and the type of treatment received. If this pain becomes chronic and it interferes with the return to normal life activities talk to your doctor.

In addition, some of the anti-estrogen drugs given to combat recurrences can cause muscle and joint pain. Some create flu-like symptoms, where the discomfort goes all the way to the bone. Some medications may affect your quality of life in other ways.

It's hard to know if the pain is from the drugs or from cancer. If your medication is causing severe pain, talk to your doctor about other options that may work for you with less severe effects. Lynn went to her doctor after thinking she had ovarian cancer. She had gone online and Googled the symptoms and freaked herself out. After speaking to her doctor and discussing the issues with one of the hormone blocking drugs she was on, they decided to try a different one and her symptoms quickly subsided.

There are several types of pain, most fall into two groups Acute and Chronic. Acute pain typically comes on suddenly and has a limited duration. Chronic pain lasts longer than acute pain and is generally somewhat resistant to medical treatment. Pay close attention to your painful symptoms and when you first noticed the discomfort. If the pain lasts more than a month, see your doctor so they can rule out cancer.

Chemobrain, or Am I Losing My Mind?

What is Chemobrain? It's that foggy feeling that clamps down over your thinking during and after chemotherapy treatment. Many cancer survivors say they have trouble processing thoughts after chemo. Some doctors deny that chemo brain exists, saying these cognitive changes are all related to the stress of a cancer diagnosis or depression. Recent studies suggest that cognitive difficulties after chemotherapy are common. Stewart Fleishman, M.D., director of cancer supportive services at Beth Israel Medical Center and St. Luke's-Roosevelt Hospital Center in New York City estimates that 80 percent of those who receive chemotherapy for any kind of cancer have some immediate cognitive changes.

Some wear the label proudly, putting on stickers and T-shirts: I've got Chemobrain, what's your excuse? But most are surprised and upset by these changes. The implications can be profound for those who never suspected they would have such trouble returning to their lives and their families. Based on studies on Chemobrain, Dr. Tim Ahles of Dartmouth-Hitchcock Medical Center concluded that *"high and standard dose chemotherapy can have a negative effect on the cognitive functioning of cancer survivors... These cognitive changes can affect attainment of educational and vocational goals and have a negative impact on the quality of life of cancer survivors."*

[3]The signs and symptoms of chemo brain vary and may include:

* Being unusually disorganized
* Difficulty concentrating, finding the right word,
* Difficulty learning new skills, or multitasking
* Fatigue
* Confusion, or feeling of mental fogginess
* Short attention span
* Short-term memory problems
* Taking longer than usual to complete routine tasks
* Trouble with verbal memory, such as remembering a conversation
* Trouble with visual memory, recalling an image or list of words

Cancer survivors may experience problems with attention, concentration, memory, and delayed thought processes. Although these issues usually resolve with time, they can be disabling. A friend of mine returned to work as a dialysis tech but her chemo brain pushed her to change careers. Her cognitive ability was compromised and the fear of making a life threatening mistake convinced her to make the change.

The risk of mental impairments from chemotherapy is greater among those who are older, have lower pre-treatment IQ, and those with a genetic mutation that is associated with Alzheimer's disease. Signs and symptoms

---

[3] Symptoms of Chemobrain By Mayo Clinic staff

of cognitive issues or memory problems vary from person to person, and are typically temporary, often subsiding within months of completing cancer treatment. According to Dr. Fleishman, for many patients the symptoms of Chemobrain begin to lift three or four months after the last chemotherapy treatment. For about 20 to 25 percent, he says, the symptoms can last five years or more, and sometimes they never go away completely.

I remember being finished with chemo and having serious doubts that I was qualified to return to work and do my job. I was very fortunate; I was able to take time off when I was diagnosed. After six surgeries and six months of chemotherapy I was scheduled to resume work. I never told a soul I was scared to death and feared my inability to perform my job after 11 months off. I remember feeling like a fraud at first, pretending everything was fine. I felt ashamed and very vulnerable. My self-esteem and confidence had never been particularly strong, but this was its lowest for sure. As a salesperson my confidence and product knowledge are what I had and, after 11 months I had neither.

Thankfully, I was able to slowly integrate back into my job, being careful to write notes for myself, so if I experienced a lapse of memory for something important, I could refer back to my notes. Slowly my memory started to improve and with it so did my confidence. Luckily, I didn't have to tell my boss or confess my short-comings and I was gradually able to rely less and less on my notes. Slowly I started to feel like I belonged in that job, but on reflection it wasn't until I started helping others that I began to really feel better; not until I started talking about how I felt, and heard other women's stories that were so similar to mine did I start to come out of my real fog. The more I talked, the more I discovered I wasn't alone in my feelings. In fact most women I have met struggled with re-entry, had fear of the cancer returning, and had to cope with the fact that cancer had changed them.

I'm Too Young for Menopause

Menopause is a normal part of the aging process for women. When it happens naturally, some women smoothly sail through and for others it's a bit bumpier ride. When menopause happens suddenly because of surgery or cancer treatment, menopause can be uncomfortable and extremely upsetting. Chemotherapy and post treatment drugs can throw a woman into menopause overnight. I remember after my first chemotherapy appointment I felt the immediate effects of menopause. The changes in my hormones triggered the dreaded hot flashes from the start. I felt silly at the time; I hadn't had a conversation with my doctor about this so I didn't understand until much later what I was experiencing. Neither my mind nor my body had the opportunity to get comfortable with the idea of menopause before I was knee deep in the side effects.

If, like me, your body was getting ready for menopause you may never have another menstrual cycle. Your body isn't the same after menopause. Weight is hard to maintain and even harder to lose. There are changes in the skin, it's like we dry up from the inside out without estrogen.

In younger women this premature menopause is often temporary and their periods usually resume months or years later after chemotherapy. In women over 40, it is often permanent. Some women, especially those with a strong family history of cancer, opt to have their ovaries removed to further reduce their risk of a recurrence but this will further intensify menopause.

Early menopause can be very distressing physically as well as emotionally. I was almost as upset about going into menopause as I was about having cancer, partly because I didn't expect it, and my symptoms lasted for years. As with natural menopause, you may experience hot flashes (including night sweats), vaginal dryness, and vaginal atrophy, loss of libido, migraines, digestive changes and difficulty thinking. It can also cause a loss of bone density and affect overall bone health. When menopause is induced surgically or chemically, these symptoms may be more severe than with natural menopause. Hot flashes and night sweats were the worst for me. They came in a wave that seemed to generate from the middle of my chest and radiate in all directions. Within a few moments I went from chilly to dripping wet with perspiration. The heat seemed to intensify for a few minutes and then slowly dissipate. At night I found myself going from a comfortable slumber under my covers to waking with a start, throwing off all the covers. The sweat soaked my sheets cooled me; I would finally drift back to sleep only to wake up again freezing cold while on top of the covers. And we wonder why we can't sleep well during treatment and after! These fits and starts of sleep did nothing positive for my attitude so I understand how frustrating life can be during this phase of recovery.

Tamoxifen blocks estrogen from binding to cancer cells, slowing tumor growth while Arimidex and other aromatase inhibitors shut down the body's ability to make estrogen outside the ovaries. Tamoxifen is generally used to prevent recurrence of estrogen receptor positive breast cancer in women who are premenopausal. Women who are postmenopausal may use either Tamoxifen or one of the aromatase inhibitors. Although aromatase inhibitors are generally better tolerated than Tamoxifen, many women find they cause joint pain which is sometimes severe.

If you postponed your natural menopause with hormone replacement therapy (HRT) then you know how hard it was to stop those drugs when your diagnosis was discovered. The adverse effects of going cold turkey into menopause are intense.

Many women seek relief for menopausal symptoms. I found using a fan at night helped some. There are now many fabrics designed for their wicking ability, so give them a try when shopping for a new pair of pajamas or night wear. Wearing layered clothing during the day so I could remove a layer or two when a hot flash manifested itself was also effective.

The good news is that there are ways to manage symptoms and live more comfortably through menopause. Your health care provider, acupuncturist, and/or naturopath can help you explore your options and find safe and effective ways to ease your symptoms without estrogen. According to Dr. Wendy Chen, Assistant Professor of Medicine at Harvard Medical School and a medical oncologist at the Dana-Farber Cancer Institute, *"Although the medical definition of menopause may be the same for all women, the symptoms and side effects for any one woman can be very different. Any treatment that is needed to calm the symptoms of menopause has to be personalized to each woman."* [4]

Carol remembers *"The doctor gave me a prescription for Tamoxifen. I began to take it and suddenly couldn't stop crying. I had horrible hot flashes and could not sleep. This went on for six weeks until I finally began to put things together. I finally realized it had to be the start of Tamoxifen. I called my doctor and the medication was changed to Arimidex which eased my symptoms."*

---

[4] http://cancer.surchy.com/breast-cancer-treatment-dr-wendy-chen-dana-farber-cancer-institute/

Where Did These Extra Pounds Come From?

I recall starting chemo thinking; *"at least I'll lose a few pounds."* Boy was I wrong! Chemotherapy immediately sent me into menopause, and by the time I went back to work 11 months later I had gained 25 lbs. Before I could go back to work, I had to buy new clothes because nothing fit. I had never had a weight problem before this. Before cancer I was easily able to maintain my weight close to my driver's license weight year after year, but not after chemo! I have lost and found 30-40 lbs. for the last 20 years. When I go on a very strict diet I can lose, then slowly but surely it creeps back on, despite being careful of what I eat. My metabolism is like a slug.

I'm not the only one. Other women also complain about gaining weight during treatment. Premenopausal women undergoing chemotherapy seem to be at the greatest risk, with a slowdown of their metabolism. [5]In fact many women have reported an average weight gain of about five to eight pounds and some as much as 25 pounds. There was my answer to this annoying problem, I wasn't the only one to deal with weight issues, but I didn't have to like it. I have struggled with this concern from my first chemo treatment.

Premature menopause brought on by chemotherapy or hormone therapy causes your metabolism to slow down. There is also a change in body composition. Your body gains more body fat and loses lean muscle. Another reason is that the corticosteroids used to help with nausea can cause an increase in appetite. They also can cause a redistribution of muscle mass from the extremities into the

---

[5] http://www.webmd.com/breast-cancer/breast-cancer-and-weight-changes?redirect=/content/article/110/109633.htm&_referer_=psychologytoday.webmd.com&orig_qs=

abdominal area as fat. That's why I have that roll over my jeans.

When Did I Become My Mother?

Aging is a fact of life, but when drugs and lack of estrogen are thrown into the mix, it seems like aging is on hyper drive. Our bodies are slowly but surely aging and deteriorating. I remember feeling like I had aged ten years overnight. One day I felt young and vibrant and the next I felt wilted, fat and tired. I remember seeing my reflection thinking, *"Who is that old lady?"* It was me.

I continue to remind myself that aging is a natural part of living and dying, but with the amount of money women spend on anti-aging potions, Botox, etc. we obviously aren't doing it very gracefully. The market research firm Global Industry Analysts estimates that a boomer-fueled consumer base, seeking to keep the dreaded signs of aging at bay, has pushed the U.S. market for anti-aging products to more than $114 billion by 2015[6].

So, when the consequences of chemo, radiation, and menopause throw us head first into aging more quickly than normal, many of us are calling foul. Aging is a normal process but I continue to buy the lotions and potions to keep my face appearing as young as possible, especially after 20 years of menopause. We all need to come to grips with the fact that we are getting older.

I have to tell you a story about a difficult birthday. I was whining and carrying on about becoming 50. It seemed sooooooo old to me. (Now that I am over 60, I wish I was 50 again, it seems young now.) Anyway, I got a call a couple weeks before my birthday from a woman who was scared to death. She had been diagnosed with breast cancer

---

[6] http://www.americanscientist.org/science/pub/boomers-will-be---spending-billions-to-counter---aging

but there was something else going on as well. Her doctor wanted her to have her ovaries removed before she started her treatment. I thought that was odd, but the doctor also suspected she had ovarian cancer and if she did, that would change the course of her treatment. She asked me to go to her doctor appointment with her when she got the results of her surgery. I told her I'd be happy to go and asked for the date to put in my calendar. She said, Sept 17th at 10:00 am. I thought, "Well that's an interesting way to spend my 50th birthday."

It ended up being a very humbling day for me. I met her and her two sisters in the waiting room and shortly was asked to go back to a small conference room with the doctor. I asked a few questions to help get clarification for her, but this lovely 46 year old woman had both breast and ovarian cancer at the same time. They were both very advanced and treatment was to start the next day. I walked away from that meeting feeling so ashamed of myself that I could whine and complain about turning 50 when this woman wouldn't ever get that opportunity. We kept in touch but her disease was so advanced she passed away less than six months later while on treatment. This was a terrible blow to me, a reality check for sure, but it continues to remind me to tap into my gratitude regularly for my health, to celebrate each birthday and to be grateful to be alive.

Aging has another element I wasn't ready for: being invisible. With our society being so youth oriented, it tends to discount those of us who are getting older. It's not intentional, but it is obvious, especially when you walk down the street in NYC with a beautiful daughter. I remember feeling odd but I did not understand what I was experiencing. My youngest lives in Brooklyn and at this time worked in the City. While visiting I would take the train to her work and ride home with her. We would stop and eat or shop, but what I remember most was walking through lots of people to get to our destination. Since I'm from the West Coast I'm used to making eye contact with people as we pass. However, in NY it's different. I began to pay attention to where people's eyes focused. Men and women on the streets were much younger in general and they didn't even notice me. Their eyes saw only my daughter. She is young, thin and pretty so that makes sense but, even though I walked right next to her, eyes almost never wandered over to me. This was men and women alike. It was a harsh reality and I didn't like it at all but it explained a lot. I decided from that day forward I would do my best to be visible, to carry myself well, and walk quickly with my head held high (until I no longer could) whether I am in New York, Paris, Oregon or anywhere.

When we stand in front of the mirror and see the changes of aging, menopause and the effects of cancer, it's time to make the choice to embrace this new body, scars, wrinkles, fat and all. The way we think about this new body, the way we carry it, is what we can control. Think about the last time you walked down the street. Do you remember seeing that person with slumped shoulders walking slowly, head down, versus the person who was holding their head up, shoulders back and walking with purpose? Who seems older? Who seems engaged in life?

If you have gained a few pounds like I did through my chemo, find a cute outfit, even if it's in a bigger size and rock it. It will add bounce to your step. Apply a little more makeup and walk with your head held high and be glad you can. Put some attitude behind that walk and be noticed. Again, it's all about attitude, and if you don't quite feel it yet, fake it until you do. That little bit of effort will start building your confidence for the future. Before you know it you will feel better too.

But I Wanted More Children

One of the most obvious effects of menopause is no longer having a menstrual cycle and then its byproduct, the inability to have children. Sometimes this is temporary, sometimes it's permanent. Younger women are at risk for infertility and premature menopause after cancer treatment, even though menses often returns. Even if the period returns, the fertility may be compromised. According to the American Cancer Society, each year more than 11,000 women under 40 are diagnosed with breast cancer in the U.S. How treatment affects fertility depends largely on three factors: the type of treatment used, type and stage of the cancer at diagnosis, and the age of the patient.

Infertility is a very emotionally charged issue even without a cancer diagnosis. Throw in premature menopause that is the involuntary result of surgery, radiation, or chemotherapy and it can surely throw a young family into turmoil. For a woman who wasn't finished having the family she wanted, facing early menopause can be life altering. I was 40, raising two step kids and I had my biological daughter at 30. Although I wasn't planning on having any more children I was angry to have the decision taken out of my hands. I was sad and found I needed to grieve the death of my youth and my ability to have children, while trying to embrace this new reality.

I've met women who were diagnosed during their pregnancy and some made other hard choices, to abort or do chemo with the baby in vitro. I met one young woman in NY who had a beautiful baby boy after doing all of her chemo while pregnant. He didn't seem affected as a newborn thank goodness but that would be a tough choice.

I'd Rather Read a Book

Breast cancer attacks our femininity, our sexuality, and our sensuality all at one time. It takes our hair, our breasts, and then menopause hits which ages us, and if you're young, disrupts fertility. We wonder why it causes issues in our sex lives. Cancer can challenge intimate relationships. It is completely normal when a partner is diagnosed to feel shocked, uncertain, scared, or anxious and to experience changes in your sexual relationship. At times you may only want the closeness but not sex, at other times you might want both, or neither. That's okay, and quite natural.

You may find that your partner has less interest in sex and intimacy as well because of physical, emotional and financial pressure related to cancer and treatment. Partners may be confused or unsure of how to best show affection and validation. When a woman has surgery she tends to be very protective of that area and then her partner is afraid to hurt her. So starts the dance.

Your partner may need some encouragement to re-engage in intimate touching near the surgery area when you are ready for sex again. Since the feeling is gone, some women can't imagine their partners even touching the scar area and pull away from their partner. Sometimes it's difficult to find a comfortable position especially if the cancer has progressed out of the breast to the ribs, back or pelvis.

Partners may be afraid of hurting you and will need permission to move forward, especially at first. The loss of nipples may also play a huge part in rediscovering what makes you feel sexy or aroused. The loss may be a constant reminder of the cancer and needs to be addressed and grieved.

One woman lamented *"The truly sad part of going through my bilateral mastectomy was losing both nipples. That was a huge erogenous zone for me, and that was taken from me."* There's not much discussion on this topic and that's unfortunate because it can be a huge issue for many women. Because they are fighting for their lives they seem embarrassed to be concerned about such things, but it is yet another loss, another scar they need to grieve.

Kathleen talked about it when she said, *"The trouble with having the second stage of reconstructive surgery for me is that most people thought, 'Okay, great, you're finally done!' But I wasn't done. I wasn't ready to tell the world I needed nipple reconstruction either. It was too intimate a topic, even for me. I have been extremely open with my family and friends about my experience with cancer and the reconstruction process. My trouble with scar tissue has delayed the progress even further, so the awkward phase has lasted longer than I care to remember. It's frustrating, but I feel way more happy than sad about my journey, even though I'm still on it and not sure when I'll really be done."*

Even the most modest woman needs to grieve the change in her breast and the loss of cleavage. Low neck fashions create a constant reminder of what one woman has and another has lost. I find it especially insensitive when a receptionist at the cancer clinic proudly flaunts her low cut t-shirt. I have watched women walk away from this experience feeling deflated and upset without actually knowing why. Women rarely discuss these non-life threatening topics with their doctors since they feel they should be grateful for life and feel silly to be worrying about such things, but they are important. We are sexual beings and it is part of the journey. The loss of, or the changes in a woman breast's may deeply affect her confidence and body image, so go slowly and have fun exploring. If necessary, create some ground rules like you did when you dated. Try only kissing, or only kissing and a little touching. Remove the goal of intercourse until it feels right. Bring back the fun and the mystery of your relationship and the intimacy will grow with time. Be patient.

I Feel Like Less Than a Woman

Cancer treatment can leave us feeling less than a woman. Whether it's the scars from surgery, the effects of drugs or radiation, none of us get out of this roller coaster without some negative feelings about ourselves. If you deal with a low libido during or even after treatment, it isn't usually a permanent side effect of cancer treatment so it can be managed. For many people, libido returns to normal after treatment ends. Since sex starts in our heads, we need to start talking about these feelings, and sometimes both parties are hesitant to get that conversation started. Many of us try to pretend and jump right back into our roles, and find those roles don't fit like they once did. Sex may have been paramount in your relationship before cancer and now it's hard to imagine taking your clothes off in front of your partner. It's okay to go slowly.

It has been reported in the research by Susan Kellogg Spadt, CRNP, PhD, *"Sexuality issues affect 90% of the breast cancer survivors in one way or another, but sadly less than one third are very frank with their healthcare providers. The two most common complaints are painful intercourse and lack of desire."* [7] The pain can be caused by low estrogen causing dryness and thinning of the tissues.

Intimacy and sex are important to most partnered relationships. Those normal parts of a relationship can be compromised with chemotherapy and/or anti-estrogen drugs. Since many of the cancer drugs are designed to stop

---

[7] Frankly Speaking: Sex After Breast Cancer

or block estrogen this exacerbates the problem. Vaginal dryness and the thinning of the walls of the vagina can all make intercourse challenging, very uncomfortable or downright painful. Because of the discomfort, your loved one may be concerned about causing you pain while being sexual, further increasing intimacy issues. Fortunately there are things you can do to help the situation. Talk to your doctor about the use of special lubricants to help with dryness and restoring proper pH balance.

Although lubricants can help with the discomfort from vaginal dryness, some women complain of painful spots that burn with intercourse that simple lubricants can't alleviate. These hot spots can make intimate relations unbearable. I discovered that I had this problem when I entered a study at OHSU with Dr. Martha Goetch, an OB/GYN at the Center of Women's Health who talked about this problem in the June 2014 OHSU blog. *"Health care providers have long thought vaginal atrophy caused pain during sex. But from my experience treating vulvar pain, I believed that the location of pain was the inner vulva, outside the vagina, and that the problem is a pain condition, not a dryness condition. I had the opportunity to research my theory thanks to funding by the Center for Women's Health Circle of Giving research grant awarded in 2011."*[8]

*"I studied 46 women with severe pain with penetration related to lack of estrogen. I focused on the area of the vulva just outside the vagina—a place where a woman can easily apply topical therapy herself. Patients used liquid lidocaine compresses for three minutes just before sex. We also provided a silicone lubricant. We found that **90 percent** could then have comfortable, enjoyable*

---

[8]*http://www.ohsu.edu/blogs/96kmiles/2014/06/20/women shealthpainfulsex/

penetration. Male partners did not note any numbing, and women had no pain—and could enjoy intimacy again." I participated in Dr. Goetsch's OHSU study and know of several others who did as well with great success.

Since our brain is the largest sex organ, whether you are done with treatment or not, consider arranging a regular date night. This will encourage time away from the cancer experience and the worries that come with this journey. Do things you both enjoy: laugh and find the joy in the little things. Rekindle activities or things you like to do together: go to a movie, go dancing, take a hike, walk around the neighborhood holding hands, or simply sit on the porch together and talk. This will allow you to put the fun back into your life and reignite your romance.

Communicate about your sexual needs. Take time to discuss your sexual relationship. What do you want? What does your partner want? These conversations can feel uncomfortable but opening up lines of communication will be rewarding. You may feel vulnerable but once you have opened the door it gets easier. Talk about the side effects of the drugs you have taken, or are taking. Talk about how your body has changed, and how that makes you feel. Opening up these tender topics will help you feel closer to your partner and make for easier intimacy. If your previous ways of being together sexually now cause pain or are no longer sexually fulfilling, explore other options. Talk to a doctor or therapist for additional ideas.

Intimacy isn't always about sexual intercourse; explore ways to share yourself in new and different methods that don't always result in a sexual encounter. Hold hands during the day when sex isn't an option. Remember flirting and verbal foreplay? We all did it when we were interested in creating a new relationship. Consider this a new relationship. Find new ways to relate to each other in and outside of the bedroom. This will build trust, intimacy and open up lines of communication. Each partner needs to be patient and keep trying.

If you have little or no desire, communicate with your partner about your lack of interest in sex. It might be awkward but keeping your concerns from your partner may leave them feeling rejected and clueless as to why you no longer desire sex. Keeping them in the loop and openly communicating about intimacy can strengthen your relationship. You may rekindle something you have lost and will find romance where routine was before the diagnosis.

It may help to know that even if you don't feel like having sex, a caring partner may be able to arouse you and help you enjoy sexual activity. It is important that you both agree on what is acceptable to each of you. Talk to each other about your worries and fears. Don't be afraid to ask each other what is OKAY and what is not. While talking about sex can be difficult, checking out each other's feelings and what you each want, can be very reassuring.

Many women and their partners say they actually feel closer to their partner after the illness. Couples facing a serious illness tend to be more attentive, stop taking each other for granted, and are grateful to have each other's support. Try to see the glass half full instead of half empty. Life after cancer may be your opportunity to remember the positive things about your relationship and your sex life rather than dwell on the negative aspects. [9]Simply touching can help you feel cared for and reduce anxiety and depression.

---

[9] Cancer Research UK:
http://www.cancerresearchuk.org/about-cancer/coping-with-cancer/coping-physically/sex-sexuality-and-cancer/how-cancer-can-affect-your-sexuality-and-sex-life

So if you have a partner, you can focus on showing your feelings for one another in other ways like:

- Enjoying being close to each other
- Touching, stroking or even holding hands
- Kissing
- Massaging
- Talking

One survivor explained it this way, *"Sometimes intimacy is a gift I offer my husband, no strings attached. I wonder about the future, what if I'm in hospice or gone. At least for today I want to offer the gift of love for as long as I can in any way I can."*

Remember to laugh together. Laughter is the best medicine sometimes. Cancer and what you have braved isn't funny, but embrace those funny moments. Don't take things so seriously, lighten up and have fun.

Chapter 4

I'm Scared to Death

The fear of the cancer returning or recurrence is an emotion we all must face. *"The treatment is done and now all I can think of is how do they know the cancer is gone? And how do I know that the cancer won't return?"* Unfortunately just like other things in life there are <u>NO</u> guarantees and no crystal balls to see into the future. When you were diagnosed it was in the plan to go for the cure unless the cancer had already spread to the bones, liver, lungs or brain. If that is the case, the doctor was going for NED, no evidence of disease. So if you are finished with treatment, consider yourself cured unless the doctor says otherwise. Could the cancer return? Yes it could, but it probably won't. That's what you need to hold on to. Please squelch any *"yeah buts."* There is always a chance it will return, but not today, hopefully not tomorrow, or next month or even next year. If it does you will deal with it then, not before. No amount of worry will change that; so don't waste your time and energy on something you have no control over and may never happen.

Still Nervous?

When the depth of the diagnosis sinks in we generally come out swinging. We amass the courage and inner strength to emotionally fight our cancer along with the doctors. When we finish treatment, cured or at least NED, we no longer have the need to fight - or do we?

"At least when the doctors were shooting poison into my veins I felt like I was doing everything I could possibly do to beat this disease. Then when treatment was finished, I felt vulnerable and exposed to the cancer again," said one survivor I worked with.

Many doctors don't do follow up scans or tests because it can give us a false sense of security, it's very expensive and the high number of false positives. They do rely on the routine mammograms if you still have breast tissue and our knowledge of what's normal in our own bodies. Your doctor will leave it up to you to tell him/her what's happening with you physically and emotionally. Your doctor needs to hear about that new pain that isn't going away or any changes that seem odd. I know it may feel like you are being a hypochondriac if you talk about each and every one of your ills, but you know your body and it's best to keep your doctor in the loop.

It's odd how we can experience these mental gyrations to deal with cancer. When I had my moments of uncertainty, I could fall back on the fact that, I was cured. This is what I tell the women I work with every day. I even go so far as to say after surgery, after the tumor is removed, you're cured; any other treatment you choose is simply insurance. When that idea sinks in, you can see an immediate physical change in their posture. They sit up straighter. A smile comes to their face as the thought washes over them and their eyes start to sparkle again. The fear and the dread subside and the dead look in their eyes disappears.

Regard all the tests and scans as confirmation of good health rather than searching for cancer. That's the glass half full, rather than half empty mindset. It's the same glass but the way we look at it or the spin we put on it can make all the difference in our quality of life. I understand that the cancer could come back, but I will deal with it if it does, and so will you.

In general terms, a five year recurrence rate of 11% is the norm, but check for your specific type of cancer. But each individual woman's risk can be different, depending on many factors including the type, grade and stage of the cancer and her treatment choices. Decide you are cured.

I Feel Like a Hypochondriac

After being released from active treatment by the doctor, initially it feels great. Then you realize you will no longer be under constant scrutiny by your medical team. It feels like you are on your own, but actually you will be seen every three or four months, then every six month, then every year because you are cured. Many women complain of feeling like a hypochondriac during this time, running to the doctor for every pain or problem after treatment has ended. I remember being fearful that cancer would come back, or in my case, I was sure it was in the other side. Since cancer didn't show up on a mammogram or an ultrasound, I couldn't be convinced it wasn't on the right side as well. I found myself being hyper vigilant with self-breast exams, finding lumps and bumps that were normal breast tissue. I went to the doctor several times when everything was completely fine, but I never felt fine. `

I laughed when a survivor told me about the pain in her big toe; she swore the cancer had come back in her toe. Fortunately, after she had it checked out she found she had arthritis, not cancer. So yes, it is normal to worry some. Unfortunately that feeling never goes away completely. It's not right in your face every minute, but I lived it too. There is a silver lining to all this worry: we do take better care of ourselves. I've talked to several doctors who say to their patients, "You will know if something is wrong." We listen to our bodies more carefully now that they have betrayed us. We can't assume they will just work without issues any longer. I believe we take better care of ourselves and go to the doctor when something "feels" off, rather than dismiss it as nothing.

I remember when I celebrated being a 15 year survivor; I started having some severe hip pain. The first thing I remember thinking, "I hope cancer didn't come back in my hip." When I comprehended how quickly my thoughts traveled back to my experience and the possibility that it had come back, I was appalled. I was 15 years out from my treatment and that was nevertheless the first thing that came to mind. The good news is, I went to the doctor, had my hip x-rayed and found out it wasn't anything I needed to worry about and in fact chiropractic solved the problem shortly thereafter. The important take away is I didn't wait to have it checked. Being a cancer survivor makes me more aware of what's going on with my body. It pushes me to take better care of myself and get things checked out rather than ignoring them. So if there is something wrong, I will catch it much earlier. So again, will you ever stop worrying completely? Probably not, but it does get better the further away from the diagnosis you are. The thoughts and concerns of the cancer returning will go back further into your subconscious and won't be top of the mind all the time. I promise.

My friend Becky had been having an odd sharp pain; it was like a shooting pain that went from her chest up the side of her neck. Her doctor had told her she would know if there's a problem. He didn't believe in annual scans just for the sake of having a scan. She mentioned this unusual new pain to her doctor. She had a PET scan and a place in the center of her chest lit up. It was an internal mammary node full of cancer, yet it was in a completely different place than the odd pain she had been having. Thankfully, the doctor was able to radiate the node and all the surrounding area and Becky has been cancer free since.

So listen to your body and talk to your doctor if something is odd. The rule of thumb from many doctors is if something persists for more than two or three weeks, it's time to bring it to your doctor's attention.

As of January 1, 2022, it is estimated that the population of cancer survivors will increase from 12 million in 2012 to almost 18 million. The overall five-year relative survival rate for female breast cancer patients has improved from 63% in the early 1960s to 90% today. This increase is due largely to improvements in treatment (i.e., chemotherapy and hormone therapy) and to widespread use of mammography screening for earlier detection. [10] Steven Castle, administrator of the Medical Center's Thomas Johns Cancer Hospital (TJCH) in Richmond, Virginia, said cancer survivors receive the highest quality care during the active phase of their treatment, but can be lost in transition to the more passive follow up phase of survivorship. *"Sometimes patients may feel abandoned or lost after their last radiation or chemotherapy treatment or their last appointment with the surgeon,"* he said.

This makes sense as people describe this time as, "waiting for the cancer to come back." The feeling that their lifeboat tether was cut when they had their final appointment, and they were let go to drift out in the medical abyss. This is where staying connected to your friends and family is so important, connecting more emotionally with survivor groups and your new sisters who have traveled this same road. It is a frightening time, but with assistance it's tolerable.

---

[10] *Cancer Treatment & Survivorship Facts & Figures 2012-2013

Connecting with Others Who Understand

I find women crave the company of other women, and support get-togethers are one place where they can mingle and share their experiences and talk about their feelings without judgment. Survivors describe a deep need for the kind of personal empathy that can be provided only by someone who's been through the cancer experience. Fellow cancer survivors can provide an understanding and can be a great source of information about what to expect from treatment and possible complications. I find them helpful as women research available resources and programs, sharing the latest trials, chemo drugs, supplements, etc. Some find simply being around other women who are living their lives gives them hope. Others find online communities very helpful, especially for those nights where sleep eludes them. One online community is www.inspire.com where no matter what time of day or night you can find someone else available to communicate. Another online group that is set up similarly to Facebook is www.mybcteam com. I also find it a great venue for those who want to reach out to others during their journey.

Patricia remembers how she felt, *"I know that my mind sets the tone for me moment to moment. Positive affirmations didn't bring any comfort. I knew that I was lying to myself when I said them. I couldn't find that emotional, mental or spiritual freedom I craved. A support group after I was finished with treatment was a Godsend. It gave me the opportunity to 'feel' my way through the fear. Acknowledging and embracing the fear brought me the gift of liberty. Just like a child in the dark cries out to its mother for comfort, I too, comforted my cries of fear. I also questioned my will to live, while at the same time I was mad at my body for betraying me."*

Research shows that survivors socializing with those who have journeyed something similar can enhance their quality of life. People who take part in support groups believe that they can live healthier, happier lives if they spend time relating to others. When women have emotional encouragement, it creates a sense of hope. It is easier to deal with their health, stress and other social problems. Some find that the bonds formed between members help them feel stronger emotionally and physically. They find sharing their feelings and experiences within these environments can reduce tension, fear, and anxiety and helps promote overall healing.

One woman I spoke to shared how disconnected she felt from everyone in her life. She had taken a break from her job to endure the first four rounds of chemo and when she went back to her employer, she found that her job had been eliminated. All the social contacts with her co-workers were now strained and uncomfortable and that arm of her emotional backing was now cut off. She felt these friends of convenience, were not friends at all and she felt alone, dejected and rejected. Her family was trying, but being scattered in other cities it was hard for them to be there in the way she needed. Her husband had been distant before the diagnosis and her cancer had put an even bigger wedge between them. But because of financial reasons she felt stuck. This woman relied on her girlfriends and new acquaintances that had traveled down a similar path. Without them her journey would have been even more scary and lonely. She found solace in the smiles of women who understood her pain. These acquaintances ended up being new friends that remained active in her life long after her treatment had ended.

If one survivor meeting doesn't fit or feels too negative, find another that better suites you or start your own. Breast Friends has taken a different approach to these gatherings depending on the needs of the group. We have some evening meetings, some breakfast gatherings, some on weekdays, some on Saturday. We even have a Happy

Hour group. We call our monthly evening meetings Girls Nite Out where everyone brings a pot luck item to share. Our monthly morning get-togethers meet in restaurants and are called Breakfast Clubs. We keep them light and positive. Each group is led by a trained survivor leader rather than the traditional hospital model run by social workers. If the conversation gets negative, we shift gears to something fun, funny or at least lighter. If you want to talk cancer, great, if not that's okay too. Our meetings tend to be more social and supportive in nature. I say this so you understand emotional support can look and feel different than the customary support group so find one that fits your needs.

When you are feeling healthier, support meetings are also a place to give back to others who are newly diagnosed, sharing your experience, and giving the insights you have learned. You might feel completely healed and ready to move on, at the same time find giving to others very rewarding. To offer a kind word and a soft shoulder while taking the emphasis off you, will benefit you as much as it does the people you help. It will give you a sense of purpose and a way to return the kindness given to you during your journey.

Cancer Is Not for Wimps

Facing your mortality is not for wimps. When faced with a life threatening disease like cancer it throws us all into an unpleasant frame of mind. The reality is we are all dying but the difference is **we,** those who have endured a cancer diagnosis, know it.

After you clock some months after the treatment phase you may look at cancer as a wakeup call. You may realize that looking face to face with the potential of dying reminds us that this life we are living is not a dress rehearsal. Even if you believe in the hereafter, this is all there is for this body. There are no do over's, all we have is the time ahead of us. We can't go back and relive our past; all we have is today and hopefully tomorrow. When that reality hits home, today is much more precious. Survivors tend to regard life differently and are less likely to take each day for granted especially for the first couple of years. A life threatening disease allows us to re-assess our priorities, our values and in general what is most important to us. Many women completely rearrange their priorities as a result of a cancer diagnosis. So when I say looking at our mortality can actually be a blessing, it may make more sense with this change in mindset.

For instance, compassionate women who love to give may find it empowering to say "No." Especially you people pleasers who take on way too much and rarely use that two letter word. It may take some practice, but it feels good. I've heard so many ladies tell me with an expression of absolute surprise, "I can say NO now." Women are accessing their calendars and matching up their activities with their values. If the activity isn't something they value, they can choose not to do it any longer. They spend their time saying yes to things they see value in, doing activities they had only allowed themselves to dream about. They spend their precious time and energy to repair broken relationships, work on deeper spiritual matters, being creative, helping others or simply to laugh more. Relationships, career plan, money, success, our health, and many other areas experience a new kind of scrutiny, a new litmus test to validate their importance and relevance in our lives.

Jan believes *"I have changed from this cancer experience and have become stronger as a person. I know that I have to do the things that I really want to do before it is too late."* This is an opportunity to create or revamp that bucket list. Do those activities that you have put on the backburner, those that bring you joy and fill you up rather than drain your energy.

Sarah recounts when she was young having a lump removed that was benign, and then worried about cancer for years. *"In spring, 1968, I found a lump in my breast. I was almost 20 and a sophomore in college. I went to the doctor on my own and he told me it would have to be removed. I went home crying and told my Mother; luckily it wasn't cancer but this was the beginning of my obsessive worrying about breast cancer. Over the next 20 years, I had several lumps that were eventually diagnosed as fibro-cysts and, with new technology, only three were removed. My children were born in the '80s and as they got older I did not worry as much, but it continued to be in the back of my mind. Guess what, in August 2010, I heard the words from the surgeon, "This one is cancer." It was a lesson I learned later in life. Worrying does not keep bad things from happening. This lesson is one of the many good things that came from having breast cancer."*

Carol remembers how both she and her husband were petrified about cancer. *"My husband was diagnosed with liver cancer two weeks after I had my mastectomies. The years of 2002 and 2003 were very tumultuous for my family. Although we had a wonderful support system, they did not comprehend the fear, anxiety and general panic we both were experiencing. My husband and I both processed our diagnosis in different ways and the whole experience left emotional scars that needed to be dealt with later."*

The fear that the cancer will return can interfere with every aspect of a person's life. Putting cancer behind you is what everyone wants but because of long lasting and or delayed emotional, social, physical and sometimes spiritual challenges can be tough. It may take much longer than originally thought.

A woman told me the other day: *"I'm sure there are many other ladies that need you more than I do since I have such great support from family and friends."* I gently asked if it was alright if I checked back when she was finished with treatment, she said yes but you could tell it was with reservations. Sure enough I called after her last chemo and she was a mess, she was scared to death, and feeling like her life no longer fit and her family and friends didn't understand. This is a very normal reaction, so if you are feeling this way you aren't going crazy, really!

This is when you need to reach out to organizations like Breast Friends, go to survivor activities, talk to social workers, connect with other women who understand what you are feeling. Managing the roller coaster of emotions will become easier. As time goes on you will be able to anticipate some of the ups and downs as you prepare for an anniversary or routine appointment or scan. You will find the tools, the emotional encouragement needed to work through the turmoil you stuffed during the treatment phase. As you read through this book you will find additional tools and coping strategies that will aid your transition to this new life after cancer. To combat some of these scary feelings, start to make plans for the future. Make short term and long term plans that help get your mind off those pending triggers that might interrupt your peace of mind. Share your feelings with those closest to you so they understand this complicated phase.

The first anniversary of your diagnosis and the first mammogram or screening test will most likely give you some nervous flutters. In fact some people are petrified. It's reminiscent of your last experience and is bound to give you some concern. Janet told me, *"It's been a year since my last radiation treatment. It's hard to believe all that happened last year and now here I am back to work, back to normal and feeling absolutely wonderful. However it is always in the back of my mind wondering if and when the cancer will return. Will it be soon? How will I know? How do I prepare if it is? How long will I have? So right now I am trying to figure out how to deal with and minimize those thoughts."*

Just remember, your doctors went for the cure unless the cancer metastasized and then they went for No Evidence of Disease (NED). Either way, consider yourself cured until you know otherwise. Take someone with you to your appointments to help focus on something other than the last time you were in the clinic. It is perfectly normal to feel a bit anxious. Don't put off your appointment because of those feelings. In fact some people talk about making it a regular celebration, create a pamper day for yourself or plan a lunch with your friends after pushing yourself to get those emotionally charged tests or appointments behind you. If the cancer is going to come back, the sooner the doctors know the better your chances of a cure and full recovery, even the second or third time around.

An article in <u>About Health</u> explains how our worry can turn to fear and anxiety and actually worsen the situation. [11]*"Worry becomes a problem when it is chronic, consuming and leads to anxious avoidance and inhibition. In other words, worry becomes fear. It distracts you from important matters, and it can inhibit action or problem solving."* Your fear can become a self-fulfilling prophecy, and that's the last thing any of us want.

Give Yourself Permission and Time to Fall Apart

Our society is full of slogans like; "Never let them see you sweat." Most of us think we need to keep it together all the time. The trick is, when a genuine problem exists, we need to express our emotions but we don't know how. Many baby boomers grew up with the proverbial

---

[11]http://panicdisorder.about.com/od/symptoms/a/worry.htm

elephant in the room and learned how to walk around it, step over it or simply ignore its existence rather than talk about it. We might use different words to convey the message, but the message is the same: don't lose it, don't fall apart, deny your emotions. Act as if everything is okay. Well, sometimes it's not.

I'm giving you permission to find people in your life who are worthy of your trust. Find people who can handle your emotions. You want folks that if you yell or cry, won't take it personally and make it about them. Perhaps you can offer a safe place for them to express their real emotions too. We all need a safe place to land. If that person is not presently in your life, use a chair or a pillow or a stuffed animal. Practice expressing your emotions. If you need to cry or yell, do it. It's important to express your feelings in constructive ways.

One client expresses herself by tapping into her creativity. She pulls out her big black pen and draws big dark circles. Sometimes she needs several pieces of paper; sometimes she adds colors. No matter the final product, when she's finished she feels better. The pressure cooker in her brain has let off the steam necessary to continue safely. Journaling can have the same effect of tapping into the right side of the brain and allow it to reduce the internal stress. Those that suffer from high blood pressure and ulcers can take a lesson from those who have found coping mechanisms to express their feelings in healthy ways and have used them successfully.

Who Knew There Is So Much Grief to Process

Grieving the losses in your life is important. When I went through the cancer journey I thought I processed the grief but the emotions that go along with losing a breast were immense. It was a very long time before I felt like I worked through all the emotions. The scars from surgery were a constant reminder of the cancer and how it changed my life. I believe when we get through the reconstruction process we feel we are finished. However, the transition from our natural breasts, no matter how large or small, no matter if they were perky or saggy, to a reconstructed breast takes time to work through and adjust. The new ones don't have the same shape, and they certainly don't act the same as the natural breast. They don't look the same, feel the same or respond the same as our natural breasts and they never will. The idea that they won't ever be the same or perfectly matched is a struggle for some to accept. We think just one more surgery and it will be better.

Improvements can be made with fat injections or using the different kinds of surgical procedures that are being developed, but the reconstructed breasts will <u>never</u> be the same as the original ones and that is the tough reality to embrace. Give yourself permission to be angry, to feel the sadness and grief. Give yourself time to cycle through all the emotions and defuse them so they don't cause more harm later.

Another topic I found myself needing to grieve was the loss of my youth. I didn't understand why this happened to me. How could I feel perfectly fine and have a cancer growing inside of me? This disease could take my life if I had ignored it. I found myself depressed, sore, sick and feeling like my youth was stolen from me. It seemed ironic to feel this way while braving a treatment that was designed to save my life. I also felt stupid and naïve. I knew I wasn't going to live forever but wow what a blow to my wellbeing. I felt very conflicted about how little I knew about cancer and its latent effects on the person diagnosed as well as their family and friends. It absolutely turned my life upside down.

Some women find they need to grieve the active lifestyle they had before the cancer and its effects. For instance you may not have the endurance to go on a long hike like you used to with a heavy pack on your back. But if you love to hike consider a less strenuous hike with less incline and shorter distance with a lighter pack to start. It may be necessary to adjust your expectations for a while until your stamina returns.

I want to say again how important it is to give yourself permission to grieve. It's acceptable to cry, be mad, punch the pillow, and overall feel your emotions. *"As a child I was always told 'Big Girls Don't Cry' and was given candy if I didn't break down emotionally. I was always praised for not showing any pain or fear. Fast forward a few decades. After dealing with cancer for five years I wish I could cry more. Sometimes I feel the tears are just under the surface. It is a pressure I want released, but don't know how,"* laments Glenna.

We all need time to work through these emotions. I'm not suggesting crying and wailing for hours on end, but I am suggesting that you take some time and if you need to cry, cry. If you need to be sad, be sad. Just don't stay there for extended periods of time. If you find yourself in this situation, it's time to call the doctor.

Create a framework that allows for these blocks of time to work through your emotions. Have your well-deserved pity party, but put a timeframe around it so you don't wallow all day, all week, or all month. If you need some time each day, take it. Many find it beneficial to work through the experience by journaling, others drawing or painting.

Others find talking about the experience helpful; I'm sure that's why group environments can be therapeutic. I found the more I talked about my experience the more I healed. The more I supported others through their emotions, the more it helped me. I would say something to console another and realize that's something I need to think about or do for myself. Buried grief can be harder to access and process later and can have long lasting negative effects on your life. So however you cope, or whoever you talk to about these feelings, get them out and then let them go.

I went to a workshop in 2015 where the facilitator helped us with letting go of negative feelings. We took a few minutes to write down the feelings we were holding on to and wanted to release. Then we gathered around in a large circle to discuss. Since everyone had their own stuff they wanted to release, we took a few moments of silence and said our goodbyes. We took the piece of paper and tore it into small pieces and then sprinkled those shards of regrets and negative feelings into the soil beneath a new tree. Our papers were going to fertilize this tree to grow tall and strong where it was being planted, while leaving us lighter without these burdens we had been holding. It was a great way to visualize and rid ourselves of these bad feelings we were carrying.

Blaming yourself is another common reaction to a cancer diagnosis. Perhaps you ignored a lump or you missed last year's mammogram. Be gentle on yourself. We can't go back. We can't change these things. All we can ask is to learn from these actions, embrace them and make them part of your story so others can learn from your decisions.

Some find it excruciating to even imagine having cancer and put their heads in the sand - certainly not the best choice but we all have our reasons. It's important to live in the present moment and know we will have some dark thoughts or times. We however, have the power to pull ourselves back. Some will need the help of friends, of faith, of some outside force. Tap into whatever it is that can improve your thinking, be more positive and in the moment.

I'm Feeling Insecure About My Future

Most of us will never deal with a recurrence. Despite the small number of cancers that return, the fear of recurrence is universal. Most women feel ill at ease after treatment ends. Cancer may seem invincible, but your doctors are trained to be one step ahead. One patient mentioned since she is a visual person she needed to draw pictures of the cancer being defeated. That was comforting for her. Do whatever alleviates the fear to understand down to your core, the cancer is gone! We don't need to continue to fight the cancer; the cancer has lost this battle.

I know some doctors hate the question, am I cured? I know some doctors are not willing to say you are cured, because the cancer may indeed return. I understand that sometimes it's a wait and see scenario, but that's when I believe that a positive mindset of believing you are cured is helpful. It can be a crapshoot, especially with the less common types of cancer, but a fearful patient actually needs that reassurance to move on.

A lovely lady in one of my Self Esteem workshops reacted strongly to my comment that she was cured. I wanted to dedicate some time to talk about her experience here. During the class we discussed some of the issues she was dealing with and her fear around the cancer. She shared that she had a small tumor with only a tiny spec of cancer in her lymph nodes. The doctor felt chemo and radiation were necessary because of the location of the tumor and how quickly it appeared to have grown. She had finished her treatment nine months before and she talked about how the leftovers from the treatment had affected her. She seemed very distraught and talked about her cancer like it controlled her body. I asked her a series of questions to get clarification and to make sure I understood what her ongoing treatment might be.

All through the workshop she talked about her cancer being metastatic so I asked more questions to make sure I understood her situation correctly since I felt like I was getting mixed messages. Finally I asked, is the cancer in your bones? NO. Is cancer in your lungs or liver? NO. I looked her straight in the eye and said, I'm not a doctor, but it sounds like you are cured. Tears of relief came flooding out. She didn't remember her doctor ever saying she was cancer free. He hadn't mentioned the fact when he dismissed her and told her he didn't need to see her for three months. She didn't know she was cured. It was such a powerful realization that even when we hope for the cure, we need to be told by our doctors, we are cured. We need to hear those words out loud.

Can her cancer come back? Yes it can come back, there are no guarantees. Is it possible, yes, but is it probable? No. With today's wonderful research, drugs, and techniques for curing this disease, the survival rates have improved drastically, and if it does come back there are numerous drugs for more advanced disease to give prolonged life. I just want to make sure we talk about this topic and if you haven't heard these words after your treatment is completed, ask for clarification. Am I cured? Make sure you understand the message the doctor is delivering. This is a great example of when the doctor thought he communicated the message, yet it wasn't being understood. Because of that, many survivors live with extra fear and unnecessary grief.

Like I said earlier, when I had my mastectomy, the cancer was gone, I was cured. The chemotherapy and the Tamoxifen were merely insurance so it didn't return. For my own sanity I needed to believe this so I could carry on. I believe this is a conscious choice that we all need to make during our journey. It's not an easy decision, but for me it was the only one that allowed me to go back to work, be the mother my children needed and live my life to the fullest.

Don't get me wrong, I had my dark scary moments where I could image I was back in the throes of cancer treatment. Many a day I felt I wasn't going to be around to see my children graduate from high school, get married, have families of their own, or start their own careers. When I would find myself in this dark and lonely place, I acknowledged my worry and concern. I made a conscious decision to move back to my present reality without cancer. I found that these scary bouts would hit me when I least expected them. They could be triggered by a song, a story that someone was telling or even a movie. Sometimes I would pick a particularly sad movie so I could cry. That way it was on my terms rather than sneak up on me when I least expected.

"To me it was so important to have someone to talk to that had gone through what I was facing. It has been six years since I went through everything and to this date I am still terrified to go to the doctor in fear that I will hear I have cancer again." explained Judy.

Most of us have these fears but they can go even deeper. Some fears are for our protection and others are not based on anything real or concrete. Some of us are afraid of dying. For my Christian sisters, what's the worst thing that could happen? We die and go to heaven? For others it might be the fear of the unknown or being afraid of the pain and suffering around dying. I know one of my fears is being a burden to my loved ones. It's painful for me to imagine how vulnerable I would feel having others care for my personal hygiene.

Another aspect of dealing with cancer is how you identify with it. Listen to the language you use around your experience; do you talk about, "My Cancer?" You are not the disease of cancer. You might have cancer or had cancer, but you aren't the cancer. Try to examine the way you talk about it, especially after you are finished with the treatment. Don't make it part of your identity. I know this is a tough one because at times it can feel like it has taken over your life, but don't allow it to be your identity. You are an amazing, multi-talented woman with things to do and places to go and cancer may dictate some aspects, but it isn't who you are as a woman. Even if you have advanced disease, remember the cancer is not who you are, it is merely something you are dealing with.

I feel the cancer won't win as long as I continue to live my life. Live life to its fullest. The fear of the future isn't worth all the time and energy it takes from us. There are no guarantees of the future after a cancer diagnosis; there were no guarantees even before cancer, we just didn't realize it.

* Cancer is Less Likely to Recur If:
- You had no or few cancerous lymph nodes found during surgery.
- It was found early and was small.
- You had adjuvant therapy (chemo or hormone therapy) along with surgery.
- You have lived 5 to 10 years without a recurrence.

*Facts about recurrence:
- Many recurrences are limited to the breast and can be completely removed by surgery.
- Nearly 33% of recurrences are found by mammography;
- About 50% of recurrences are found by physical exam; and
- About 20% are found by both methods.

- About 75% of women who treat a local recurrence by having a total mastectomy are disease-free 5 years later.[12]

Cancer has forced you to be self-focused to get through all the bumps through the cancer but at some point it will be time to get on with your life. This is a conscious decision we all need to make after this long journey. I have found that the best way to get over myself, is to help other people. It never fails when I am in the depths of a pity party, if I open myself up to others, I will find someone else in more pain. Someone else's cancer is worse than mine or that has metastasized. Perhaps they have added circumstances like being in the midst of an unwanted divorce, their parent was just diagnosed with dementia or their kids are doing drugs and need rehab.

Being a sounding board to others allows you to get out of your head, and put your focus on someone or something else. Another way to refocus your energy is to volunteer for an organization that you are passionate about. If animals are important to you, volunteer for a no kill shelter and help the homeless animals find permanent homes or offer your time at your local veterinarian office. These kinds of activities allow you to be more grateful for your life and even your problems.

What I have covered are the primary emotional and physical side effects. In all of these and any others you experience either in treatment or after, please consult your medical team for ways to medically treat these issues. Our medical personnel are dedicated to cure the cancer or reduce its progression. They are searching for ways to reduce the harsh effects of the drugs and discomfort you feel. However, until greater strides are made in this area, it is up to you, the reader, and the patient, to understand your

---

[12] *Per Susan G Komen for the Cure.

need to speak up and to be your own advocate. This is your life, take responsibility for it. Educate yourself rather than take everything at face value. Ask questions and expect answers!

Chapter 5

How Do I Feel Normal Again?

Deborah states it nicely when she said, *"I'd like to say that I enjoy and appreciate life more now than I did before cancer, but that would be too simplistic. I did learn some lessons about appreciation and love, but I must admit that I am more anxious and worried than I ever was before cancer. I worry for myself, for my daughter, and for my whole family. I've had five women friends my age die of cancer in the last year. I feel that my innocence has been taken from me due to cancer. I do feel that each day is a chance to do what you really want to do... there's no need to put it all off for some later date. I also understand pain and healing like I never knew before. I am so amazed by the body's desire to heal and recover. That has been a wonderful learning experience."*

Terri says, *"I think most people thought when treatment was over, it was over. I was fine for a while after the treatment was completed. My hair started returning and I was feeling as though I looked 'normal' again. But something was off emotionally. I wasn't able to either address it or understand it for a while. I finally decided to seek some professional help to overcome the anger I had been hanging on to that I was unaware of."*

How Are You Coping?

Part of the process of feeling normal again is to understand there is no normal, really. This new you is a

118

culmination of who you were before the cancer and this new mysterious you that needs to be figured out.

The desire for our lives to go back to the way they were before our cancer diagnosis is very strong, but unfortunately, not realistic. Many of us won't ever be the same physically, mentally, emotionally, or even spiritually, but that doesn't have to be all bad. The memory of the trauma and the ordeal we have endured will start to fade, I assure you, but it will never be as if the cancer didn't happen. Be confident it will get better. Until it does let's talk about the best ways to cope. I have come up with a mnemonic that might assist you with this process.

C.O.P.I.N.G
C- Compassion for yourself and others
O- Optimism toward your future
P- Preparation and Planning
I- Information and Education
N- New perspective and embrace what is happening now
G- Get moving toward new goals and living

Observe each of these areas and think about how they measure up in your life. Compassion for yourself and others is foremost. Be gentle on yourself. Give yourself time for this transition and the understanding that you won't wake up one day and find the cancer experience behind you. It just doesn't work like that. This can be confusing for us as well as the others around us. Choose optimism for your future. No one has a crystal ball to know what the future holds, but you do have a choice on how to see and experience the journey.

Self-Compassion

Drawing on the writings of various Buddhist teachers has operationalized self-compassion as consisting of three main elements: kindness, a sense of common humanity, and mindfulness. [13] "These components combine and interact to create a self-compassionate frame of mind. Self-compassion is relevant when considering personal inadequacies, mistakes, and failures, as well as when confronting painful life situations that are outside of our control."

Self-compassion is how we treat ourselves. Most women are wonderful caregivers. They give their time and energy to others but don't understand how to take that same care and time for themselves. I remind my ladies regularly to be kind to themselves. If you haven't learned how to be kind to yourself before now, a cancer experience will give you a great opportunity to practice. Some women push back and tell me it feels selfish. I try hard to dispel the myth that taking care of ourselves is selfish, but I will agree it takes practice. When our giving reservoir is empty we feel resentful, exhausted and depleted. If we don't take the time and energy to replenish ourselves, resentment, anger and illness happen. It's important for your personal happiness and wellbeing to practice filling up your tank. After you do, you will find you are more able to give to others in the future.

As adults we may not have had self-compassion modeled for us and so we will need to become the parent and the child to instill in ourselves the importance of this practice. An example of being gentle on yourself and the use of self-compassion is to examine how you talk to yourself and imagine saying those same things to a good friend. Are they appropriate? Would you say them in the

---

[13] (e.g., Salzberg 1997), Kristen Neff (2003b)

same way to your friend as you do to yourself? For instance, if you forgot an important appointment, you realized it too late to get across town and make the meeting. You feel embarrassed, and at that moment what do you say to yourself? I am so stupid, why do I do these kinds of things? Or do you make a quick phone call, apologize for the mistake, figure out how the mistake happened so it doesn't happen in the future, then move on to the next task on your list. It is possible to take responsibility for the mistake and remain compassionate to yourself. No one is perfect, we all make mistakes. Analyze what happened, what could you have done differently? If you see where your responsibility lies, it will be easier to not repeat the behavior again. Honestly critique the *behavior*, but not your character.

Some people recharge their batteries by being near the water, some by experiencing nature, some by being alone and some by socializing with others. Figure out what gives you energy and plug this activity regularly into your schedule. This can be tricky if your special time is having that alone time and you live in a busy household where the only time you have to yourself is in the bathroom, and even that's compromised. If you have a lock on the bathroom door, pampering yourself with 30 minutes in the bath may be one way to give yourself the gift of silence and recharging. If you have a hard time getting a few minutes to yourself, start paying attention to your boundaries or lack of them. We will talk more in detail about boundaries later.

Part of self-compassion is also being open to receive; many find it easier to give than to receive. Receiving may make you feel uncomfortable, or even vulnerable. This is partly because we don't get kudos or rewards for receiving, or we don't want to be burden or indebted to another. Because of this and other reasons, we don't know how to accept the generosity of others. One of my greatest fears is to lose my independence as I age. The thought of being reliant on anyone, family, friends or even a paid caregiver is terrifying to me. The thought of being a burden to someone makes me nauseous. The funny thing is I remind my patients almost daily how important it is to accept assistance when it is offered. I do believe if I need to learn something important, I learn it more completely if I teach the concept to others. That way when I hear it coming out of my mouth over again, it reminds me to be more self-compassionate.

By allowing others to help you, you are giving them a gift. When we give to others it makes us feel good. When people offer to do something nice or generous for us, it feels good to them as well. A personal example is this book. I mentioned I was writing this book during a Thriving Beyond Cancer retreat I was facilitating. One of the participants, Michelle, offered to work with me. She had written three textbooks that were published and she offered to edit my manuscript. My initial thought was why would she want to do such a thing for me? After many conversations I grasped what a gift this was to me, but it also was a message that she felt passionate about and wanted to see it reach the women that need it. We have worked together for a couple of years and I am appreciative for her selfless efforts.

So when others offer to assist me I try to remember this principle so I accept their generosity understanding they are enjoying the opportunity to help. It's not always easy, but it's a worthwhile skill to develop. By allowing others to help you get what you want, it will renew your spirit so you will be able to give more in the future.

If the cancer is advanced and it has metastasized to another part of your body, life can be more difficult. Even so, you are breathing, you are alive, so give yourself permission to live, not simply exist. Tell yourself the cancer is being managed and hopefully under control. My philosophy is if you are still around you have things to do. I believe there is a plan for us all. It may not be clear or easy to decipher but it's there. Perhaps it is to model for others around you what courage looks like, or it's time to find your higher power. Whatever it is, be the best you can be until you can be no longer.

Be Your Own Health Advocate - Be a Squeaky Wheel

Whether we are talking about your physical health or your mental health, you need to be your own health advocate. Your life may depend on it. As a cancer survivor most doctors are really tuned in and will listen to your concerns. If you have concerns, make sure you get your questions answered. First thing, don't panic. Hopefully, whatever you are feeling is nothing serious. It may be residual from your treatments or the anti-estrogen pill you are taking. With all you have endured it is normal to have some anxious feelings about every twinge or pain. That is normal. If you have something that doesn't resolve itself within a reasonable amount of time, talk to your doctor about your concerns. If that pain or odd feeling continues being a problem after a few weeks to a month, go to your doctor. Don't assume when you feel a pain or a new sensation that something is wrong or the cancer is back. Pay attention; mark it on the calendar when you first noticed it and observe if it gets worse. If it does resolve itself, that's great, but if it doesn't you have very specific information for your doctor. You know your body best. It's important to pay attention so you can articulate your concerns. If you rush to the doctor and say something vague like, "I have a pain," that isn't very useful all by itself and your medical team will need more information. If you say, "I started noticing a pain under my right arm three weeks ago. It's sharp at first and then fades to a burning sensation," you may get better results and your physician can move toward an answer to the problem more quickly.

When you can explain where the pain is located, is it a burning kind of pain, a stabbing kind of pain, is it all the time, only when you move a certain way, etc. your doctor will have a better idea where to start and rule out your worse fears more quickly. If you come prepared for your appointment and give the doctor what he or she needs, you are more likely to walk away feeling heard and more confident.

If you feel there is something wrong and you aren't being listened to after waiting for a month and giving them helpful information then this is when the squeaky wheel comes into play. If they said they will call and they don't in a timely manner, call them. If you are waiting for test results and they haven't called to let you know the results, call them. And keep calling them until you get some satisfaction. It may not always be the news you want but if it is bad news the sooner you move on it the better the ultimate outcome.

If you and your doctor are not communicating on the same level, talk to the clinic manager and see if there is another doctor more suitable to your communication style. Not all doctors are created equal. Most are brilliant, wonderful doctors but may not be able to communicate a complex topic where the layman understands. I believe medical professionals want to heal you and want you to feel better.

Come prepared with a list of questions so you can come right to the point and get all your questions answered. Ask clarifying, multilevel questions so you can get to the answers you need if you don't understand the initial answer. For a list of questions for many of your doctor appointments, go to the Breast Friends website at https://www.breastfriends.org/support-services/patients-and-survivors/recently-diagnosed/quest/.

If you don't ask questions, they will presume you understand what has been said. Ask them in several different ways and if you continue to have trouble understanding, talk to someone else. It is important you understand all they are telling you. If you are really unhappy, it's reasonable to find another medical provider to take care of you. Understand that there will be a transition period with any new doctors to build the trust necessary to know you and your situation and to get used to your communication style.

One patient shares how she took control of her healthcare choices. *"It would be easy to just give up and let my medical team plan my care, let my church friends pray for me and allow my family to decide for me on the next course of action. I had fallen into this trap and later regretted the choices I allowed that were contrary to my personal input or preferences. If something goes wrong, it is easy to blame those that you allowed to make the choices for you. But don't be the victim. To consent to serious cancer treatment requires being fully on board with the choice of care. If you go kicking and screaming into the unknown, I don't believe your body can respond to healing the same as if you made a carefully chosen choice to go with the program; this applies to traditional and complementary treatment. You must be at peace and believe that you have made the best choice possible.*

To achieve this level of peace you may need to ask a doctor to delay a treatment for a day or two while you emotionally work through what to do. You may need to withdraw from family and friends for a weekend of solitude. If you practice listening in silence, you can learn to hear what the next step is that is right for you. Dealing with cancer never leads to cookie cutter choices. Each person is different and has their own pathway to wholeness that is unique to them. I believe that since I have started to embrace the fact that I am responsible for my health I have felt more empowered, more at peace, more ready and willing to move forward with the discipline that is required to make life altering changes."

Finding the Positive

When things are not going the way you want, it is easy to concentrate on the negative. The tendency is to focus on what we've lost, what we miss about the life we had before cancer. Refocus your attention from what you have lost to what you have. What may I learn from this, how can I use this experience to help others. Concentrate on what continues to work and is positive in your life and your relationships and build on those gifts.

An example of a negative I wanted to embrace is my being forced into menopause without warning or discussion by my oncologist. I was not happy, but finding positive aspects was helpful. I don't have periods any longer and I don't have cramps and bloating or PMS. I don't need to buy tampons or pads. I was rarely cold during menopause with the hot flashes and since I had always dealt with low blood pressure, being cold was an everyday happening. You get the idea, even in a less than positive circumstance there are positives if you are willing to search hard enough.

Let's try a new approach and find the positive things about your body. Make a list of all the things you **like** about your body. Don't forget things like your smile, the color of your eyes, how your body digests and processes food properly. I know this sounds funny but only after I talked to a lovely ovarian cancer survivor who spoke to me candidly about her journey did I appreciate that I can go into the bathroom and everything works properly. She dealt with an emergency surgery for a kinked bowel and came out with a temporary colostomy. Fortunately, after about three months she was able to go back into surgery and have it repaired and things got back to working order.

Because of this experience I think about my normal routine body functions very differently than before. I appreciate the fact my plumbing works without me thinking about it. Sometimes we need to dig deep and think about the things that are working and be happy for those things. Examine what's right, not what's wrong. Make a list of what's right.

Only after you're finished with the list of what's right, create a list of the things you would like to change, but don't be harsh on yourself. Which things do you have control over? The things you can't change, like the scars from that surgery or the shape of your nose are most likely not going to change unless you have a line item in your budget for a plastic surgeon. Embrace those things you cannot change. They make you, *you*. The aspects you do have control over like standing up straighter or smiling more can be improved with practice.

Below are three examples for each list, but please write as many as possible, especially in the positive category. Come up with at least as many positives as negatives.

Things I like about myself   (Example)
1. Smile
2. Shape of my head
3. How clear my skin is

Things I don't like about myself   (Example)
1. Width of my hips   (Ask yourself is it bone structure or a few extra pounds?)
2. Big feet   (can I do anything about this?) No
3. Flabby stomach   (If I exercise and lose a few pounds I could improve this one.)

Take some time and think about your lists. Why do I like the things on my positive list? Have I worked to improve or change these things in the past? Are they God given traits or attributes? Am I grateful for the gifts I've been given? How could I process and accept the things I can't change? How can I change those things I do have control over? Remember the Serenity Prayer.

Serenity Prayer
Reinhold Niebuhr (1892-1971)

God grant me the serenity
to accept the things I cannot change;
courage to change the things I can;
and wisdom to know the difference.

You Control the Food and Exercise

Some women blame themselves for their cancer diagnosis: I didn't eat well enough, I didn't exercise enough. One survivor told me she created a list of all the reason she got cancer. *"I'm overweigh, I eat red meat, I buried my emotions, I lived next to a military base as a child, I live a block from a cell tower. My list went on and on, but who knows what actually caused the cancer?"*

Another patient remembers how she blamed herself. *"I did start to collect a list of causes I thought I should blame myself for. I gained extra weight. I ate too much meat. I ate too much junk food. I held on to negative feelings for too long. I did not exercise enough. I did not do deep breathing enough etc. etc. The question of whether each point was true or not was not as important as the fact I blamed myself for each and every one. Soon I was buried under a mountain of shame and guilt. Then thoughts like, 'you don't deserve to get better,' entered in. 'You are a bad person. You have no self-control. It is your entire fault that you are sick.' Each of these thoughts carried their*

own burdensome cargo as they went through my mind like
a train.

It is easy to stand back and see how destructive
these thoughts can be. I am learning to change my self-talk
to include, 'yes, this may be true, but I did not know.' My
personal growth was not at the point I needed it to be when
I made those choices. Now, I choose to forgive
myself. Today is a day of new choices."

Another lady I spoke to wanted validation that the
Diet Coke she drank on a regular basis was to blame for her
cancer. I explained that while sodas are not healthy for us,
and perhaps contribute to obesity, there is no evidence at
this time that soda causes breast cancer. I tried to convince
her that she had not caused her cancer by drinking Diet
Coke, unfortunately, she was not to be deterred. She was
hell-bent to blame her cancer on something, otherwise it
just didn't make sense to her.

I can understand the need to know why we get
cancer; perhaps if we knew why, we could keep it from
happening or from coming back. Unfortunately, it doesn't
always work as it seems it should. I have met many young
women who are fit and healthy who are diagnosed with
cancer. They do everything right; they eat right, exercise,
keep their stress levels down, and they nonetheless get
cancer. And then others drink too much, smoke, don't
exercise, don't eat healthy and they don't get cancer.
Sometimes there is no rhyme nor reason why the body
functions the way it does. It seems like it simply stops
working one day long enough for a cancer to grab hold and
start causing problems.

We can't control or change a moment in the past,
but you can at least influence the future. I'm not suggesting
that what you eat, or if you exercise regularly, will
guarantee a cancer-free future; it can however reduce your
risk and make you feel better while you are enjoying your
new choices. In general, take good care of yourself.

Understand that what is normal today may be different than normal was before cancer.

The highest risk factors for breast cancer are two things we can't control, being a woman and getting older. You can however, control many other cancer risk factors like:

- Keep weight at a healthy level, lose or gain weight if necessary.
- Get daily exercise
- Stop smoking
- Moderate alcohol consumption

Many breast cancers are estrogen fed and our doctors do everything they can to remove or at least block that estrogen with surgery and drugs. Unfortunately those extra pounds, especially those around the middle, not only store estrogen, but our fat cells manufacture estrogen. So having extra belling fat can compromise the efforts of the anti-estrogen medicines we take after formal treatments.

Another interesting bit of research released in 2014 suggests *"Recurrence of hormone-related breast cancer was cut by half in overweight and obese women who regularly used aspirin or other non-steroidal anti-inflammatory drugs (NSAIDs),"* according to data published in *Cancer Research*, a journal of the American Association for Cancer Research. More and more research is improving our understanding of ways we can reduce our risk. [14]

It is recommended you eat more fruits and vegetables, more whole-grain breads and cereals. Don't starve your brain of complex carbohydrates. Eat fewer high fat foods, less red meat and less fried foods, since they are leading sources of fat. Also, eat less processed foods and

---

[14] http://www.ncbi.nlm.nih.gov/pmc/articles/PMC3178267/

sweets such as cakes and cookies. Eat a diet of moderation. I'm not a dietitian so if you need assistance with specific diets or diet recommendations, please consult a trained professional. On the other hand, I do know that for most people, if we overload our bodies with too much sugar and too much fat it makes our brains sluggish, we lose our creativity and our ability to think straight. So control your intake. A balanced diet is one of the keys to feeling better and achieving your goals.

Although the evidence for taking dietary supplements is mixed, I'm a believer in taking vitamin supplements because of how our foods have been compromised with modern farming techniques. I feel regular supplements aid my body's health. My immune system tends to be weak. If I go two weeks without my vitamins I get whatever happens to be going around, cold, flu you name it. I take my vitamins daily to make sure I am giving my body the extra dose of what it needs to be healthy in addition to eating healthy foods.

In 2015 there has been a lot of interest in vitamin D. The Vitamin D Council, a nonprofit organization in California, states that *"studies have shown that there is a link between low vitamin D and breast cancer. Women who have breast cancer tend to have low levels of vitamin D in their blood. Women with higher vitamin D levels are less likely to develop breast cancer. Women with higher vitamin D levels who have breast cancer tend to have smaller tumors and are less likely to die from breast cancer."* [15] Vitamin D can build our immune systems, improve our mood, and seems to have some connection to breast cancer.

Another important part of healthy living is balancing the energy you take in with the energy you use. Physical activity not only uses energy (calories) but

---

[15] http://www.vitamindcouncil.org/health-conditions/breast-cancer/

reduces the risk of some types of cancer. Your body needs to move. Take a walk several times a week, bicycle around the neighborhood. You will see things on foot or pedaling that you miss while driving your car. I'm not an athlete. I was the last one to be picked for athletic activities in school, so I associate exercise with those painful memories. I'm not particularly good at anything physical, but I can walk around my block, and then I can walk around my neighborhood. The point is you don't have to do it all at once. Take baby steps to move off the couch and get your blood pumping. You will feel better after you do.

You might find you enjoy it and want to do a bit more. Join a walking team, start running, and train for a 5K. There's even a phone app called, Couch to 5K in eight weeks. Start the process with those baby steps, we all have to start somewhere. Build physical activity into your daily routine. Do whatever physical activity you enjoy most and one that will get you moving - dancing, hiking, riding a bike or playing with the kids. After exercising, think about how good you feel about yourself and your body. Use that to motivate yourself the next time.

Even though it is counter intuitive, exercise also improves stamina and decreases fatigue. I've heard so many times women say they are soooo tired they can't get off the couch. Exercise has been proven to reduce fatigue. Exercise also decreases the depression and sadness associated with cancer. The hardest part is starting. A friend reminded me that the first step was merely to put on her walking shoes, then put one foot in front of the other.

While on your walk, notice and enjoy the sights, the smells, and the sheer beauty of the outdoors. Be present, in the moment and you will find the sights much more enjoyable. I'm fortunate to live in the suburbs where it's green and full of trees. Then even when I walk while visiting my daughter in Brooklyn I find it enjoyable. I play games with myself and see alphabetical letters in this urban setting in fences, poles and buildings. I am in the moment and enjoy the environment, graffiti and all. Avoid thinking about all you need to do when you return from your walk. I take my camera at times so I can record those first sights of spring or a bird I haven't noticed before. This also keeps me in the moment.

All these things will reduce your fatigue and boost your mood. This kind of activity can be fun. Find someone to walk with you, a neighbor or a friend. Keep the conversation positive so it's something you want to do more often. Make a plan to walk each day or at least three days a week. Even on those days where you feel especially tired, or you just don't feel like exercising, if you have someone to be accountable to, it will push you out of the house and move. We all need an accountability partner, someone we don't want to disappoint. Even on those tough days I wouldn't bail on a friend if she was counting on me to be there. It's a great motivator to keep me going.

Overwhelmed and Stressed

Stress is another element in which we have some control. Stress affects our quality of life now and our risk for cancer recurrence later. Stress and anxiety are secret killers; they break down our immune system and allow diseases like cancer to take hold. Our bodies are designed to be relaxed most of the time. We have a warning system that kicks in when we are afraid or upset. When we call on our fight or flight response too often, it can cause damage.

Unfortunately, many of us with all the pressures of life remain in the fight or flight level most of the time. Dr. Lisa Rankins' research shows how *"your body's natural self-repair mechanisms - the ones that help prevent heart disease, fight cancer, ward off infection, and assist in anti-aging, get flipped off when under stress. As far as your body's health is concerned, thoughts, beliefs, and feelings that trigger the stress response may damage your health more than a poor diet, avoiding exercise, bad habits, and sleep deprivation."* [16]

Since stress tends to break down our immune system we need to be aware of how our life is trending. I have found so many people where the cancer diagnosis is merely one of the many stressful factors that have happened in their lives. In fact, it's the end of a string of tragic events like caring for an elder or losing a parent. These pressures weaken the body's natural ability to fight.

When our immune systems are compromised there tends to be inflammation. Dr. Max Wicha found, in a study published in the 2009 Journal of Clinical Oncology, that lower cancer survival rates correlated with higher levels of inflammation. [17]

Stress is something we can't get rid of completely but we can reduce it, whether it's in our jobs, our homes or in our relationships. Assess where the lion's share of your tension comes from in your life and find ways to change or limit those activities. I have had women in high stress jobs rethink their positions and the importance of their health in comparison to the joy it brings them and/or money they get from those positions. Manage your stress rather than having the stress manage you.

Smoking and Alcohol

According to the American Cancer Society *"Even a few drinks a week is linked with an increased risk of breast cancer in women. This risk may be especially high in women who do not get enough folate (a B vitamin) in their*

---

[16] https://www.youtube.com/watch?v=gcai0i2tJt0
[17] http://www.prevention.com/health/health-concerns/breast-cancer-new-treatments-prevent-cancer-recurrence

diet or through supplements. Alcohol can affect estrogen levels in the body, which may explain some of the increased risk. " [18]

Much discussion has been around the benefits vs the negative aspects of drinking. Harvard Health Publication Blog from Harvard Medical School mentions *"If you are at high risk for coronary artery disease and at low risk for breast cancer, a drink a day could be beneficial. If you are at high risk for breast cancer, then drinking alcohol might do you more harm than good. And keep in mind that alcohol affects almost every other system in the body besides the heart and breasts. With all the focus on the benefits and risks of moderate drinking, excessive drinking is often overlooked. The National Institute of Health estimates that 4 in 10 people who drink alcohol are heavy drinkers or at risk of becoming one, and that nearly 19 million Americans have a problem with alcohol."* [19] Many studies have shown that high alcohol intake increases the risk of cancer.

I had the pleasure of listening to a professional speaker about this subject. She had an enormous wine glass, about four feet tall on the stage with her. She, tongue in cheek referred to her one glass a day policy and brought down the house as she lovingly referred to her glass. I try to live by the philosophy of drinking in moderation. I will have an occasional drink, but not every day, and not even every week. An occasional drink isn't likely to kill me, unlike smoking.

I think we all know smoking can cause cancer: If you smoke, stop! According to the CDC, cigarette smoking is responsible for more than 480,000 deaths per

---

[18]http://www.cancer.org/cancer/cancercauses/dietandphysic alactivity/alcohol-use-and-cancer

[19] http://www.health.harvard.edu/blog/study-supports-alcohol-breast-cancer-link-201111033747

135

year in the United States, including more than 41,000 deaths resulting from secondhand smoke exposure.[20]

I know that's easier said than done but no matter your excuse: The social part of it, it tastes good, it keeps my weight down, it curbs my appetite, it calms me down etc., none of this matters if you get cancer. This is one thing you can control. There are many ways you can stop smoking. Investigate them and choose one that sounds most plausible to you. Between patches, gum, electronic cigarettes, hypnosis, to name a few, many people have been successful in quitting this deadly habit. I'm not suggesting it's easy, but it is necessary to reduce your risk of cancer. And, if you've tried to quit before and failed, don't beat yourself up, simply try again. On average, people quit smoking five times before they finally become a permanent nonsmoker.

Focus on What You Can Change

When you focus on the positive instead of the negative, things indeed do change for the better. For instance, if all I can think about is how something bugs me, how it makes me crazy or really grates on my nerves, it will get worse and worse. Whatever we think about, we draw closer to us. Years ago I was so tired of my job; I couldn't see anything good about it. I didn't think I could endure it one day longer. I was angry at management because they overlooked me for several promotions. I felt disrespected and was clearly unhappy. I started to search for another position outside the company; one that I felt was worthy of my loyalty, hard work and my talents. I wanted a company

---

[20]https://www.cdc.gov/tobacco/data_statistics/fact_sheets/fast_facts/index.htm

136

that would appreciate me and give me the title I felt I deserved.

It wasn't more than a couple of weeks, and I found it! I interviewed, and sure enough they wanted to hire me. I was so excited. I wanted to give notice and jump right into their arms. But because I had 17 years with my present employer, I wanted to weigh the pros and cons before I made such a big move. I needed to think seriously about this decision so I didn't make a big mistake. I spent the next few days considering the work I would be doing vs the work I was presently doing. I considered the time I would need to ramp up in the new position, which was also a new division in the company. I thought about the flexibility I presently had because of my tenure, including personal time off, and vacation time earned. With small children that flexibility was invaluable.

To my surprise after a few short days of considering the pros and cons of both jobs I realized I truly didn't want this new position. I found that when I examined and understood my core values and what was actually important to me, the new job didn't measure up. I reconsidered my present position and I understood what I would need to give up and I wasn't willing to compromise my time with my children. I made the conscious choice to see the positive parts of my present employment and stay put, and be happy about it. I remember going back to work after making this monumental decision with a completely different attitude. The funny thing was the job hadn't changed a bit; my boss didn't change, nor did the company philosophy. It was indeed the same job I left on Friday. But on Monday because of my change of attitude and the way I now saw my job, I appreciated my employment in a whole new way. I could work my 8-5 job, go home to my children who were young at the time, and not worry about the job. I could enjoy the flexibility of the job and take that vacation time I had accrued… the list went on and on. It was huge! It was a much better job when I changed my attitude. When I was resentful all I could see were the bad or negative things about the job, but when it was my choice to leave or stay most of the negatives melted away.

This works with marriages, friendships and children as well as doctors, nurses and other medical staff. If we look for the negative in a situation or in a person, that's what we will find. If we look for the positive, that's what we will find.

So now let's do an exercise to find the positive in our cancer experience. It's easy to find the negative, as we know, so now let's shift gears and focus on the positive. Most everything should fit into one or more of these areas. As we run through the exercises I want you to keep these categories in mind.

1. Relationships/Family	2. Emotional
3. Spiritual	4. Social
5. Physical/Health	6. Financial
7. Mental	8. Job/Career

Linda points out even though cancer wasn't a pleasant experience positive, things do emerge. *"There is some fear and anxiety every time I get a mammogram. When I feel a twinge somewhere in my body, not just in my breast, I think of cancer. Cancer was a bad time in my life and definitely a bad experience, but there is some good from my experience too. I feel an incredible bond with anyone else who's had cancer, especially someone who has a new diagnosis. I understand their feelings of fear, confusion, frustration and concern about financial fallout."*

Let's think about cancer from a new place. We all know the crummy things we've lost or how the cancer has affected us from the negative angle. Now it's time to see the cancer from a positive one. It might be easier to find the positive aspects of cancer in some of these areas more than in others. Stretch your thinking around even the most difficult area.

For instance, cancer can be devastating financially. Keeping up on the co-pays or the deductibles can cause financial ruin, but look for any glimpse of positive. Perhaps it may have been the catalyst for the family to review their budget and figure out creative ways to trim or eliminate waste and manage money more effectively. That's an example of how to find the positive, even in a tough situation. This exercise is an important step to see the cancer from a different perspective. This mind shift will help you find other more positive aspects to focus on rather than dwell on the negative parts. I want you to examine each of the eight areas and write down at least one positive in each category.

Take a piece of paper and answer this question:

How has cancer affected your life **positively** in these areas?

1. Relationships/Family
2. Spiritual
3. Physical/Health
4. Mental
5. Emotional
6. Social
7. Financial
8. Job/Career

All of the exercises in this book are very fluid, meaning you can do them over and over again. As you heal, your answers will become more positive. The answers may also come more easily. As your circumstances change, your outlook and goals will expand.

If you are feeling stuck in some of the areas, share the exercise with others and allow them to make suggestions you can agree upon. Michelle reflects after finishing her treatment, *"Cancer helped me stop and take inventory of my life. It helped me make positive life changes. It showed me that I am stronger than I ever thought possible."*

Everything is a Habit, So You Can Change Anything

I remember going to a workshop and walking away with the biggest "ah ha" moment when I realized everything we do is a habit. Therefore I have the power to change anything about myself that I don't like. I am a visual person. I like to have my things visible, if they are out of sight they are out of mind. I tend to make piles of stuff on my desk, on the kitchen counter and near where I work on the couch, etc. After grasping it was merely a habit I knew if it is important enough to me, or bugged me or others enough I could change that habit.

Some are good habits and some are ones that served us at one time but perhaps not now. If everything is a habit, we can change them all. We can change how we think and change how we act by making the decision. If a behavior is no longer serving us we can change it. It's a choice, for instance, if I say, "I'm just a grumpy person, you know how I am." Others are supposed to tolerate being around me and accepting me as a grumpy person? No, actually being grumpy is a choice and a habit that can change. Not all habits are easy to change, but you can work on them and change that grumpy nature to a more positive one with some effort. Or I bet you know the person who says, "I'm just not a morning person, you know better than to talk to me before I had my morning coffee." Maybe it's you? Again this is a habit. Examine why you're not a morning person. Do you get enough rest? Do you eat late at night so your body is processing your food rather than getting the sleep you need, etc. Whatever it is, you have the power to change those behaviors if you choose. No one makes you cranky in the morning except you.

We've all heard the definition of insanity, doing the same thing over and over and expecting a different result. Well, it's true. If we keep doing the things we always did, we will continue to get the results we always have. So it is our choice to change what we don't like about ourselves and our surroundings. To find the positive rather than the negative is a habit that can be improved if you practice.

This isn't like in the movies where, poof--you are different. This is going to take some work. If you tend to be Negative Nellie and you want to be more like Positive Polly, you can change things, but it takes time and effort and that means not doing it perfectly every time. The experts talk about how a habit takes a minimum of 21 days to break, but it's merely about creating a new habit to take its place. If you tend to respond negatively, stop yourself, think about the words and practice rephrasing it more positively. Be aware of the negative thoughts. Start the process of rephrasing those negative thoughts into more positive words. It takes close to a month to acquire this new way of thinking. Practice listening for negative phrases. Reframe them and speak a more positive version. With time and effort you will start to automatically think and speak more positively. Just like any habit, we can relapse. Any smokers out there? Changing a habit may take some additional work past the initial few weeks, but you will be off to a good start. Nicotine is actually out of your system in three days, the rest is emotional addition. Awareness and desire to change is half the battle. Go for a walk, eat an apple instead of lighting up.

What habit do you want to change? Since this section is about the body, perhaps there is something there to work on? List a few ideas you want to tackle.

Chapter 6

Where's All the Money Going?

When thinking about cancer and all it affects, the cost associated with appointments, treatments and tests tend to bubble right to the top of most people's financial worries. Even with insurance, the co-payments and deductibles can create an uncomfortable burden. A recent survey conducted by the Association of Oncology Social Work (AOSW) shows that more than one half of cancer patients indicate cancer costs negatively impact their focus on recovery.[21] The cost of treatment may take a while to sink in, but when it does it can change the focus from recovery to how are we going to pay for everything. Some patients find the financial burden overwhelming and may affect their willingness or ability to finish prescribed treatments, potentially changing overall survivor outcomes. Start putting some money away now for possible health issues in the future.

I remember complaining to my doctor one day about the high cost of my chemo pills. I had gone to the pharmacy and picked up my prescription for the pills I took every day for six months. These were on top of the chemotherapy infusions every two weeks. The pills alone cost over $250.00 per month. I had insurance that covered all but a small co-pay. I asked my doctor, what do people

---

[21]http://www.socialworktoday.com/archive/032210p14.shtml

do if they don't have insurance? She looked me straight into my eyes and said without hesitation, "they die." My heart skipped a beat I'm sure, I could hardly breathe. I remember that conversation like it was yesterday. Fortunately things have improved dramatically since my diagnosis in 1993 in my state with the Oregon Health Plan and now nationwide with the Affordable Care Act (ACA).

Even with the uncertainty of our future healthcare most insurance companies and Medicare cover the cost of diagnostic mammograms and subsequent treatment if necessary. And, in many parts of the U.S., low-cost or free mammograms are offered through national programs and community organizations even without insurance.[22] Check in your state how programs work to assure coverage in the future. It's still not a perfect system but with more conversation, around the importance of this issue more lives will be saved in the future.

With the advent of online crowd funding and fundraising programs *like https://www.gofundme.com/* or *http://www.giveforward.com/p/cancer-fundraising,* a whole new way to help cancer financial issues has opened up. Have someone help you create a profile and send out the emails, thousands of dollars can be generated by generous donation of friends and family. If the electronic avenue isn't of interest, the old fashion fundraiser works, bake sale, rummage sale, car wash, just be creative. When friends and family ask how they can help, here's another idea.

Money may still be tight and so a budget may help you get your arms around your financial situation. Many of us don't know what we spend month to month and so it's a great exercise to utilize even if it's temporary. Knowing what all your expenses are, what you can reduce or eliminate and what must stay or are constant would be a

---

[22]http://ww5.komen.org/LowCostorFreeMammograms.html#sthash.jgu8Ptzv.dpuf

huge step in the right direction. Estimate medical expenses, copays and out of pocket expenses. Estimate income sources and if they don't balance out, create a plan. Most of your creditors will work with you on lessening your monthly obligations if you explain your situation and be proactive.

Ability to Work

Many patients try to continue working but not all are able to keep up the pace, depending on how severe the treatments, overall health and the effects of the treatments. Consider the physical and emotional demands your employment places on you. Consider the time off you will need and even periods of lessened productivity you may encounter. While in treatment you will have reduced energy. Your employer needs to get the job done, so when you know, give them an idea on your treatment timeline. Keep your human resources department in the conversation. They will understand if the timeline changes but it can be helpful for planning. Side effects of the treatments can vary from person to person. Knowing the potential residual effects of treatment will help you and your employer manage how it might affect the job. Your healthcare team can be a great resource and serve as allies through this process. Speak up and voice your needs and desires during this time to both your employer as well as your health care team.

Some cancer patients don't have a choice to not work, especially those who are self-employed or those that don't have a second income to rely upon. With the flurry of doctors' appointments in the first few weeks after diagnosis, as well as the emotional turmoil, working especially full time does become tough. Even if you are fortunate to have an employer willing to adjust your hours and your work load, the loss of income can cause upheaval in any household.

Sarah remembers her decision to work through her treatment, *"Co-workers become family and supported me with daily affirmations of how strong I was and the lesson my strength was teaching others by my presence on the job. Little did they know the job was saving me."*

Talking to Your Co-Workers

Talking about the cancer with co-workers may help. When you open up to those who care and explain what you are experiencing, it can be used as teaching moments. Your friends at work will better understand the challenges you are facing and how they might help. Whether you choose to tell co-workers or not, there will be discussion about why you are gone or missing so much work. The new chemo induced hairdo is a dead giveaway and will always lead to speculation when you return. Personally I suggest you tell those at least closest to you and allow the rest to hear it through your friends. My feeling is I would rather them know the truth rather than makeup something.

Caringbridge.com is another helpful option to tell many people at once. It allows you to electronically explain, update and inform all those in your network at the same time with the same information with the least amount of effort on your part. I think it's important to hear yourself tell the story a couple of times so you can grasp it yourself, but it gets old really fast to tell it over and over again. The ability to do it electronically will limit the number of updates that are necessary without slighting anyone who wants or needs to know. You can create a post and all who have signed up to receive them will be notified at the same time of the latest news. There is also a calendar for those interested in helping with rides, dinners or any other chores you list that you or your family may need during this time.

If it's too late for that, keep it in mind for the next person you know who joins the club.

My Employer Thinks I've Been on Vacation

Going back to work after time off can be another obstacle. Employers may not understand how treatments affect overall fatigue, stamina and ability to return to work. I've had some women say their employers acted as if they had been on vacation and should be refreshed and ready to hit the floor running. Employers want you to be 100% when you return to work. It will depend on several things like the kind of work you do and how the treatment has affected your overall health. Some people may need accommodations, lighter work load, shorter work hours, etc. when transitioning back to work. Some patients find they need more rest, or need to return to work part time to build up their stamina. Talk to your employer openly about your situation to accommodate your needs and theirs.

I remember when I went back to work, my stamina wasn't great so I went back half days to start. I laughed about my need for my afternoon nap, but in reality it wasn't a laughing matter. I needed that break in the day to be able to keep going for the rest my shift. I went to bed many days at 7-8pm depending on the needs of my kids. So my suggestion is to have a plan in place that both you and your employer can live with. If you feel better than you think, you can always accelerate the plan. It's much easier to increase your hours than reduce them once you are back to work. Remember this is your life and the quality of that life is important. Work and being productive is certainly one element to life, but it isn't everything. Take care of your health.

Even if we are physically healed it will be a long time until we are 100% emotionally healed. With that being said, our employers still have the right to want the job done. Like we talked about earlier, possible accommodations may be available, but there comes a time to put the cancer behind you.

Just like friends and family, your employer most likely doesn't understand that you are not the person you were when you left for cancer treatment. Your performance measurements will be based on never having been ill. Because of this it is important to communicate with your employer, HR department or direct supervisor about what is going on with you and if there are things they can do to make this transition easier for all involved. Obviously they need the job done and you need the job. So being candid about how the whole experience has affected you may be helpful for everyone.

I worked for a large corporation for 21 years when I was diagnosed. I was very fortunate to qualify for short term disability. I had 38 weeks of full pay and several more weeks at 60% until I returned to work after 47 weeks. My HR department helped me with the paperwork and explained my benefits. Find out if you qualify for short term or long term disability. I have since purchased supplemental insurance with Aflac (after being cancer free for 8 years) so even though I have changed employers I would be covered if I have another health crisis.

Now that I have been helping support women emotionally for many years, I have met many who have worked though their treatment, I can see advantages to both. For me there was a downside to being off work for that long. I remember having way too much time on my hands during the day when my children were at school and my husband was at work. I had worked full time since I was 18 years old after I graduated from high school and part time for four years before that. I was comfortable working and other than taking eight months off when my daughter was born, I had been working 8-5 type hours forever. So having all this time was actually very depressing for me. I had way too much time to worry about the cancer, about dying, and about what my children would do if I did die. I was relieved I could stay home and get the rest I needed, but I didn't get the social interaction I needed or craved.

Our confidence can take a real hit during this phase. Being away from my job for nearly a year made me feel like the world had moved on without me. I was amazed at how many things had changed. I had trouble remembering how to log in on my computer. My memory was fuzzy from the chemo and side effect of menopause. I remember wondering, will I ever feel confident doing this job again? I wasn't comfortable feeling like this. I didn't tell anyone how I was feeling. I felt panicky to think my secret inadequacy would be discovered. I needed my job. I needed my insurance, especially now. I felt like a fraud. I hoped those feelings would go away soon and I could fake it long enough to get back the confidence I once had. Fortunately, with time and a few creative tools like writing everything down to help me remember, I felt better in a few months.

Some women find their jobs less fulfilling or less important than they once thought after looking at their mortality through the cancer lens. Many find petty co-workers and work without purpose and passion no longer worth the energy to endure. Terri remembers going back to work and how it was received by her co-workers. *"My co-workers were always supportive while I was off work and in treatment, but after I was done, I worked a 6 hour day for a while and I could feel a little animosity from them."* Another gal mentioned how she felt responsible for her work environment falling apart after she was diagnosed. She felt as if the other workers blamed her for getting cancer.

Know your Rights

Many working people with cancer don't realize or know their rights and may be protected under state and federal laws. Learn about these rights to make sure you are not being discriminated against and receive the accommodations you are entitled to. This knowledge can serve as a tool to voice the best solution for all involved. If you are dealing with job problems related to cancer you may be protected by federal laws like the Rehabilitation Act and the Americans with Disabilities Act (ADA). Under the (ADA), an employee with more than 15 employees must make a reasonable accommodation for workers with a disability, as long as this does not impose an undue hardship on the company's business. Undue hardship is defined as anything that requires significant difficulty or expense in light of the company's size or resources. The employer is also not required to lower quality or production standards in making the accommodations. The Disabilities Act prohibits discrimination in hiring or firing employees and in the provision of benefits. Reasonable accommodations that should be made for employees with cancer include changes in work hours, time off for medical appointments and side effect from treatment. Most accommodations for workers do not cost money and if they do, the amount is usually very low.

Some employees will also benefit from the Family and Medical Leave Act (FMLA). This law lets many people with serious illnesses or those caring for a loved one to take excused unpaid leave. Family and Medical Leave Act (FMLA)[23] pertains to companies with over 50 employees. Under this act the company must allow 12

---

[23]http://www.cancer.org/treatment/findingandpayingfortreat ment/understandingfinancialandlegalmatters/americans-with-disabilities-act

weeks of unpaid leave during any 12 month period, and it requires the company to continue to provide benefits including health insurance during the leave period. The employee must be allowed to return to the same or equivalent position after the leave. FMLA also allows leave to care for a spouse, child, or parent with a serious health condition and for a reduced work schedule when medically necessary.

Ask if your company has an EAP (Employee Assistance Plan) as part of the benefits package. You may be able to see a counselor, or tap into other resources you might need. EAP's are designed to help employees and their families resolve a wide range of issues that may arise with the cancer experience. It's important to understanding what's best for you to heal and get back on your feet again.

If you take a medical leave and then return to work, remember you have the same rights as anyone else in the workplace. You should be given equal opportunities in promotion and how you are treated in the workplace should depend entirely on your abilities and qualifications. As long as you are able to fulfill your job duties, you cannot be fired or penalized for being sick. Talk to your human resources department or another workplace expert for more information that specifically will impact you and your position.

Protecting yourself is important so if you have any questions read "*Be Prepared – The Complete Financial, Legal, and Practical Guide to Living with Cancer, HIV, and other Life-Challenging Conditions* written by David S. Landay or *Living and Working with Cancer Workbook* by Cancer + Careers.

Understand your company's policies around these topics. Contact your human resources department, read your company handbook and understand your rights. Ask the questions; get the answers so there are no surprises.

Part 2

Chapter 7

My Worst Nightmare Came True

If the cancer does return it is not your fault. Cancer responds or doesn't respond to treatment, it's all in the biology of the tumor and how your body responds to the therapy. The way I think about it is, you've done it before you can do it again. It's not something any of us want but at least some of the scary aspects, like the fear of the unknown, are reduced since you have gone down this road before.

A Second Diagnosis

It could be a recurrence or it could be a second new primary that has nothing to do with the original cancer. Either way it's not an easy journey to face. Many women say that facing cancer the first time was one of the hardest things they have ever endured. Women who have a second cancer or a recurrence of cancer often feel angry, yet become resigned to the idea. The fear of the unknown is one of the toughest fears to deal with the first time around. Not knowing how the surgery will go, not knowing how we will react to the chemo, losing our hair, etc. At least you now know more about cancer, have a better understanding around its language and what to expect.

Stay in the moment and don't worry what's behind the next bend. If you are getting ready for surgery, research that, and only that. Refrain from worrying about the chemotherapy you may need later. Make one decision at a time rather than overwhelm yourself with multiple decisions. This will keep you in the present and feel more in control of your emotions. I love the quote by William Ralph Inge, *"Worry is interest paid on debt not yet incurred."* [24] If worry helped the cancer go away or not return, then I'd say so, but it doesn't.

My friend Becky found out eight years after her first bout that she had cancer in the other breast. It had nothing to do with the first side. After the second cancer she decided to have a double mastectomy. The pathology showed the original cancer side was perfectly clear. The lumpectomy, chemo and radiation had cured that cancer eight years before. She had developed a second new primary on the other side.

She called me from the parking lot of the clinic and confirmed my fears for her. This call however was calmer and more under control than the call I got eight years before. She said, *"You know how we always say nothing is worse than getting the diagnosis of cancer, except if you get that diagnosis again?"* She went on to say, *"It's not as bad. Not that I'm looking forward to going through the whole ordeal again, but the fear of the unknown is gone. I know I got through it the first time, I can get through it again."* It was great to hear that perspective and be able to pass it along to others facing a similar situation.

_____

[24] http://www.cleverquotations.com/quote/800/worry-is-interest-paid-on-debt-not-yet-incurred

Chapter 8

I'm Metastatic, Now What Do I Do?

If the cancer returns and it's metastatic, meaning it has popped up somewhere outside the breast. Being stage four does change things and is a whole new ball game. It doesn't seem fair that a disease you fought so hard to destroy would come back and could be even scarier. As my dad used to say, the only thing in this world that's fair is the weather. Cancer leaves us feeling very vulnerable, but it won't win as long as we continue to live, not just exist. Live life to its fullest. Even if you need to treat it like chronic disease, you can endure it. Even when worry creeps into your mind, never give up hope that you will live a long life. Make a conscious decision to move forward and be all you can be, with or without cancer. Make a plan for treating the cancer if it comes back. Find a survivor group with women who understands metastatic cancer.

Hearing you have cancer is life changing. When those words also include that the cancer has spread to the bones, the vital organs or the brain that is not only a game changer, its life threatening. In fact, how you play the game changes too. Instead of the doctors going for a cure, they are hoping to manage your disease. They want the disease to go away, but statistics suggest that the cancer will most likely come back. When my friend Becky was diagnosed the third time she said, *"This may be what takes my life someday, but not today."* As of this writing she is healthy, cancer free and is busy traveling, speaking, writing and helping to run Breast Friends with me.

Some of us are diagnosed at stage four at initial diagnosis. Some later if the cancer returns. It's never easy to hear these words but I think it would be much harder to hear at the initial diagnosis. There is no time to get used to the idea of having cancer, let alone cancer that is metastatic and not curable. The treatments may be similar to what we've had in the past or they may be completely different. With metastatic disease we don't know if it will go into remission this time or if this is the beginning of the end. That's where the scariest part manifests itself.

Some women feel so scared, sick and alone they don't feel capable or informed enough to make treatment choices. One of my patients recalls returning from her doctor so overwhelmed she couldn't function. Feeling completely helpless, she sat in the middle of the floor, with tears streaming down her cheeks, searching blindly for surgeons in the yellow pages.

No matter what stage we are when we are diagnosed we think about death or dying. The facts remain unless you are stage four; you are not going to die if the cancer remains in the breast. It's when it moves to a vital organ, like lungs or liver, to the bone or the brain, that it becomes more worrisome.

Metastatic or advanced cancer can mean so many things. If a cancer has moved to the bones or to an organ, then it's considered metastatic or "Mets." I know a woman who has lived for 30 plus years managing her disease. We worked together but because she was very private. I never knew she had dealt with hot spots in her lungs for years. I truly didn't understand what that meant until I had my own diagnosis. Her cancer had gone to her lungs and every once in a while the cancer would raise its ugly head and need some attention. She dealt with it and went on and lived her life. As of this writing she is still enjoying a productive life.

Many women with Mets to the bone find they can manage the progression with bone strengthening drugs, radiation etc. Like I mentioned earlier, the doctors aim for no progression and if possible N.E.D. It's not a cure, but patients can live a lifetime without progression or even being managed like other chronic diseases.

Glenna remembers, *"I will never forget that day. My oncologist dropped his head, lowered his voice, and without eye contact told me I had stage IV Breast Cancer. It had metastasized to my bones. Perhaps he had given the diagnosis too many times. Maybe he was weary or just sad for me. I don't know. But his reaction left me overwhelmed and on a slippery slope emotionally. If he did not have hope, how could he give me hope? I needed hope."*

If you are diagnosed with stage four metastatic disease it can throw everyone into a tailspin for a while until the full extent of the disease can be evaluated and the treatment begins. It forces the one diagnosed, as well as everyone around her, to think about the potential of death and dying for real this time. It takes a subject that normally stays in the closet and places it smack dab in front of us on the table. Very few of us are comfortable with these topics even though death is inevitable. I'm not saying everyone diagnosed with advanced disease will die of cancer but the chances unfortunately are greater. We all will die of something, but in our culture we tend not to discuss death until it is imminent.

With all the advances and research being done, many metastatic patients are being treated as a chronic disease rather than the death sentence it was in the past. So, don't give up, but be smart and think about the future realistically. Preparation and planning is taking care of business. As your head clears from the news, you will feel better and have the strength, both emotionally and physically to make plans. Create your will, your family

155

trust, your living will and advance directives, and your burial plans. Think about what goes to who, make those decisions, have those conversations, and then move on to living. Get all your wishes written down and then forget about them. Live the life you have been postponing. It's time to take that trip, visit the grandkids, pull the bucket list out or create a new one that reflects the things that are important to you now. That way, no matter when the time comes, there will be no regrets.

Many women must deal with cancer as a chronic disease. There are some days when it's a struggle. Other days being around people allows them to forget they have cancer and live normally. The doctors manage the disease but it's up to us to manage our heads, especially on the days when we don't feel well or lack the necessary energy. It's up to us to take advantage of the good days and not waste them. Make plans and if necessary cancel them if the timing isn't quite right. Don't stop planning because you <u>might not</u> feel well enough, or cancel because you <u>might not</u> feel up to it. Always have something to look forward to, fill that calendar so you have a future. I'm not suggesting running yourself ragged but instead maintain a comfortable pace where rest, relaxation, friends, family and self-care are built in to the schedule along with personal activities that bring you joy. Keep adding to the bucket list as you mark off your accomplishments.

Joyce is metastatic and doing well. She lives alone and finds she sometimes needs someone to talk to about the topics and decisions she faces. She doesn't need someone to make the hard decisions for her, rather to help her think things through so she can make her own best decisions. Having someone to bounce things off of when dealing with medical questions, how to deal with future housing, property and possessions make these daunting issues more manageable.

I remember inviting Jan to participate in our Bald is Beautiful photo shoot. She's the sweetest gal, with a great attitude but had mentioned not feeling very good about the way she looked these days. This new round of chemo did leave her bald again and I knew posing in front of a camera might be pushing her comfort zone a bit but thought it would be something she would enjoy. Several years ago she had a double mastectomy, a lot of chemo and then finished up with radiation. Unfortunately, her cancer came back in her bones a few years later so she had even more radiation. I remember seeing her blackened skin as she changed her shirt for the photo shoot. Her arms were swollen from lymphedema and she had a few stubbles of hair on her head which had started to return. Her makeup was professionally done, adding the eyebrows that were missing and false lashes that really made her eyes pop. I watched the photographer pose her and get her to smile. Before long she was having such a good time. It made me so happy to watch the transformation.

When she finished the photo shoot her smile was still affixed to her face and she was beaming. I walked over to her and gave her the biggest hug and told her how beautiful she was. She held on to me and said with tears streaming from her eyes, *"I can't tell you how long it's been since I've felt beautiful."* We both cried and hugged for a longest time. The photos turned out amazingly well, where her inner and outer beauty came to life. It was such a gift for me to be able to witness her makeover and feeling that she was truly beautiful. No matter our age or our situation, we all want to feel beautiful, to feel normal, and to feel cared about. This photo shoot took place over one short afternoon, but the effects will last her lifetime.

Stage four cancers or metastatic disease is frightening even for the strongest person. It's tempting to put your life on hold in anticipation of the worst. We have met women who have been given a terrible diagnosis and

157

prognosis, and seemed to be waiting to die. Several years later realizing they didn't die, and were well past their "expiration date," wondered what happened to their dreams. They finally chose to live again.

Years ago we hosted a Young Metastatic Support Group at Breast Friends. I remember being so taken by one woman who came on a regular basis and shared her life and her quest with inflammatory breast cancer with myself and the group. She was in her early thirties and while she was pregnant with her first child she started having a problem with an itchy rash on her breast. The doctor prescribed a topical ointment that helped but it never really went away. After her baby was born she had some additional doctor appointments and it was discovered that she had inflammatory breast cancer, a rare type of breast cancer that doesn't have the normal lump many of us experience. This rash was on the skin and unfortunately in her situation the cancer had already moved past her breast into others parts of her body, thus receiving the dreaded stage four diagnosis.

She came to the meeting every month and described her life. Her life was full of doctor appointments and caring for her daughter. She described how her life felt on hold while her husband's moved forward. He worked out of town much of the time so she felt like a single mom and resented him. Her main concern of course was their young daughter. I remember her coming to the realization that she had allowed cancer to consume her life. She never believed she would live this long, but she had. She recognized then, she had put her life on hold. She merely existed from one chemo to the next or from one scan or the next, finally waking up to realize five years had passed and she was still alive.

This was a good lesson for her but also a great lesson for me. I now relay this situation to others who are so afraid of progression in their disease or afraid of its return that they stop living. The disease may come back or even get worse, but then again it may not. So live each day, anticipating what joy may be present rather than living under that black cloud.

But You Don't Look Sick!

We know how losing your hair can be devastating, but in contrast, many of the chemotherapies that are most effective for metastatic disease don't affect your hair. So if you have advanced disease you may appear fine to the rest of the world. It seems kind of strange to me that a person who could possibly die from this crazy disease continues to have hair and look healthier than those women who end up completely cured and are bald for months. The drugs are designed to work differently but, for most people baldness is the telltale sign of having cancer. Again, this is something I had to learn and so will your network.

I think it is a natural tendency to believe it's not as serious if you haven't lost your hair. That is definitely not the case, but again, until you live this life, most of us don't understand this reality. If this is your situation, it's up to you to discuss and educate those closest to you so they do start to understand. They will appreciate your insight, your candor and your honesty. You can make a difficult conversation more palatable by broaching the topics in a straight forward manner. People want and need to ask questions but don't want to offend, upset or overstep their bounds, so they don't say anything at all.

Unfortunately not talking about these tough subjects can put additional strain on any relationship. That extra strain is the last thing we need during this time. We want and need our loved ones to understand and step up when we face an advanced cancer diagnosis. We need people to get comfortable (as much as we all can be) with this difficult situation and that only happens when you are willing to be vulnerable and open to your feelings and willingness to talk about the hard stuff.

Some patients choose not to disclose their diagnosis because they are worried that they will be treated differently. They don't want their friends to feel sorry for them or disappear altogether because of fear. They need people in their lives to be authentic with instead of feeling the need to pretend they are fine. They may need assistance to get their affairs in order. Be that person, and then go one more step by encouraging them to set aside their prognosis and live their life to the best of their ability. Having dreams and a plan for the future gives us all something to look forward to, whether it's as simple as a week-end trip to the beach, or celebrating a birthday or anniversary, or as big as an extended vacation to someplace you've always dreamed of going.

Don't be afraid to talk about the future. Buy those airline tickets; add the few dollars for insurance if necessary but plan that trip and make it happen. Have several things planned, things to anticipate, with the understanding that fatigue may slow you down sometimes, but it doesn't have to take away your dreams.

"Even when we don't look sick, we may be doing a good job of hiding our pain," said one woman I helped. Understand we all need each other to get through this life and leave the kind of legacy we deserve. Medical advances have been able to prolong even the worst cases.

Met's is the New C Word

Some mets patients must undergo treatment for the rest of their lives. Their priorities become very clear; they don't do anything that's going to hinder them physically or emotionally. They must purge negative people out of their lives to remain positive. We all could take lessons from those who understand they are dying. They aren't dying tomorrow, but they know they are dying all the same. Not like the rest of us who think there will always be a tomorrow to do the things we want to do eventually.

A stage four patient talked about her anxiety around her failing health and the little ways she takes control and is able to calm herself. *"For me little actions help, warming a blanket in the dryer and wrapping up in it, pulling out the hot water bottle, or making a cup of hot tea. Even if I don't feel like drinking it, the warmth in my hands is calming. It is a time for quiet pleasant conversation. This is not the time to discuss family relational dynamics or budgets. Quiet music and dim lights help. Often this is when I turn on the TV and watch old reruns of The Walton's or Little House on the Prairie. Shows that are sweet, safe, and slow are the best. This is not the time for tense or sad dramas. Nor is it time to solve mysterious murders. I also keep simple puzzles of twenty five to fifty pieces by my chair. I do word find games. Both are little tools to keep moving through the waters of anxiety. It helps to know the anxious fog will pass. I don't need to analyze it or focus on it. I simply dog paddle until it passes."*

Jesse reminded me *"I have been through one round of hormone therapy, eight rounds of chemotherapy and three sessions of radiation. My cancer has spread from my breasts into my liver, my bones and my brain. I have been in and out of studies and have had 4 full years of treatments. I have traveled. I have spoken to many, many others about their cancer paths and hopefully helped them along the way. I have an active relationship with my God and give thanks to him for each and every day. I have amazing family and friends that support and buoy me up every day. I am exhausted. Tired to my core and no amount of sleep revives me anymore. But I fight on every day."*

One of my metastatic patients taught me a very good lesson, now I pass on to others. *"Early in my cancer journey I was given a word of wisdom. I was just starting radiation after my lumpectomy. At this point I wanted to do anything to get better, no matter what. I allowed the medical world to dictate my every move. I would often have five or six appointments in a week. It seemed my primary care doctor, oncologist, physical therapist, radiation oncologist, all wanted to see me in a single week. I was using Medical Transport to and from my appointments. One driver was an older man from Ethiopia. He seemed kind and attentive. So one day I struck up a conversation with him. I said "What did you do before you came to America?" He said he was a pharmacist and had owned a Pharmacy in Ethiopia. Then he said something that really impacted me.*

'Ma'am, May I give you some advice? You Americans do not understand healing. I pick you up and drop you off day after day. In my country we understand that if you are sick you need to rest in order to heal. Take my suggestion and reschedule your appointments so you also have healing time.' I thanked him and had the courage to take his advice. I had fallen into a trap of seeing my medical team as having total control over my life. So I took back the control of my schedule.

I continued with my treatment plan, but I learned to speak up and say, 'No, I can't come in next week. I already have three appointments that week.' I learned not to schedule doctor appointments two days in a row. Having a day off in between appointments helped me rest. After all, on an appointment day I needed to get up, get dressed, plan my day, go out into traffic, be around people in a waiting room, complete painful treatments, make decisions about my care, and take in new information from the doctor. All of these activities could be draining.

I had the courage to phone my oncologist and say that they had to reschedule my IV. I was not coming in on my wedding anniversary. I would need a different day for the appointment. If two doctors wanted to see me at the same medical center then I asked the receptionist to look for a date where I could see both of them in the same day so I would not have to travel to that location twice. If I needed four or five days to just get out of the city and sit in nature, I considered this part of my healing and moved appointments around to accommodate the time away. I look back on that word of advice by the Ethiopian pharmacist and am thankful for the freedom and sense of control it gave me over my healing journey."

No Pity Looks, Please

That look of pity in people's eyes never feels good. Unfortunately, many don't know any better and don't understand the impact of how it makes us feel. Sympathy is feelings of pity and sorrow for someone else's misfortune where empathy is being able to imagine yourself in someone else's shoes. If you haven't walked the walk, most people don't understand the nuances of empathy and the difference between the two. They give you sympathy, or that pity look, or the "poor thing" cock of the head and think they are being helpful. If you are like most of the women I talk to, the last thing they want or need is sympathy. The more people understand the differences between sympathy and empathy, the more effective communication will become. The better the communications, the more satisfying their relationships will be in the future.

No one really wants to have others feel sorry for them, but we do want empathy. We all need a person in our life that gets it, someone who really understands without much conversation. Someone who can sit across from you, hold your hand and feel what you are feeling. When we have personal experience, we have a different perspective from those who have not lived the experience firsthand.

This can allow many to communicate in a way that feels warm and accepting rather than laced in pity.

I received another great learning from a gal who was given six months to live. She told me candidly that there are many great lessons about being able to be real and transparent with close friends and family during this time. The hardest part was when it was time for the visit to end. *"It felt like I must say my final goodbyes each and every time they left my side. Since neither one of us knew if this was the last time I would see them, they would cry and get very upset. I found I was always reassuring them so they could feel better about my dying."* The learning for me was how important it is for the patient to be honest and vulnerable and because she shared her insight with me, I can share her wisdom so others can understand the burden placed on the patient. The last thing any of us want is to make this transition more difficult. I felt humbled and honored to learn this lesson in such a loving way.

Few of us are skilled in talking about serious illness or death and dying. Most go around in a state of denial until its right in our face when we don't have any other option than to face it and talk about it. Until we educate those we love and those we associate with, we will continue to receive the look. I know this adds additional burden to those braving the journey, but until our society embraces serious illness and death along with the process of aging this isn't going to change.

Considering Assistance with Finances

Money is one of the last topics right alongside of dying we consider taboo to share with family and friends. As complicated and time consuming as these issues can be, have a trusted friend or relative help you with paperwork and finances. Just filling out insurance company paperwork can be daunting and takes the little energy you have while fighting this disease. Lay it all out so those trusted people have all the information they need to help you navigate the maze. Allow them to do some research on your behalf to see what programs you may qualify for now and in the future.

There are some little known tips to help with other financial situations. For instance, if you have life insurance in place when diagnosed with advanced cancer, there may be a way to tap into the policy to help you with your finances now. Talk to your insurance company to see if they have a program like this. You may be able to extract money from your policy before your death.

If you are dealing with metastatic disease, you may qualify for social security disability. It takes several months but generally if dealing with stage four cancer you are within your rights to apply.

Review your medical insurance policy so you know what your plan covers and where you can take full advantage of its provisions. Understand deductibles, copays and co-insurance if you have it. You may be asked about family history and genetic testing. Look for hidden benefits that will cover physical therapy, counseling, in home health care or other services that might be a benefit during this time. There may be conditions where experimental drugs may or may not be covered. Know your options before you need them.

Talk to the hospitals and cancer clinics financial departments to negotiate a reduction of your billing. If you're hurting financially and know you need to leave your job even temporarily, go to your local social service department and apply for medical assistance, food stamps and temporary disability. Some patients are not eligible for these services but if you don't ask for the services you need, you for sure won't get them.

If you lose your job, cut your hours or you are unable to work, find out how COBRA works and if you qualify. Do I qualify for Medicare, Medicaid or Veteran's benefits? Does my hospital use Hill-Burton Programs that offers free or low cost services to those unable to pay. What do I qualify for?

If I Don't Work I Will Lose My Insurance

Many don't realize that the list of expenses for a cancer patient doesn't only cover specific treatments, but everything from doctor visits and lab tests to hospital stays and home care, which can add up to tens of thousands of dollars.

A 2010 study by the National Cancer Institute[25] estimated that the amount of money Americans spend on cancer treatment each year would increase 27 percent between 2010 and 2020, to reach a staggering $158 billion per year. And having medical insurance doesn't eliminate all out-of-pocket expenses. A 2011 Duke University medical study[26] surveying 216 cancer patients found that average out-of-pocket costs for treatment exceeded $700 a month; despite the fact all but one of the participants had health insurance.

For someone who is regularly fighting a civil war with their body, these costs can be crippling and can result in patients not following recommended treatment procedures. Some patients in the Duke study reported not filling prescriptions, rationing medications, skipping treatment appointments and opting out of recommended tests in order to save money.

---

[25]http://jnci.oxfordjournals.org/content/early/2011/01/12/jnci.djq495.full

[26]http://corporate.dukemedicine.org/news_and_publications/news_office/news/medical-bills-force-cancer-patients-to-skimp-on-care-and-necessities

Metastatic Disease is Complex

One patient explains, *"For a time after I learned I had stage four cancer I simply stopped dreaming. I felt like I lived on a dead-end street with nowhere to go. I used to love thinking about traveling to Switzerland or other far off places. Soon I could hardly imagine a trip to buy groceries. I quickly learned that hope and dreams go together. Little by little I have dared to dream again. I still can't expand my dreams too far, but I have learned that planning and anticipating a three day trip to the Oregon coast is very therapeutic.*

People talk about their 'Bucket List.' I really don't care for the term. It seems too final. Like what happens if you finish your list? I think looking for happy and pleasant things to do can be an ever expanding list. A Google search on the Internet for fun activities will come up with expansive and creative lists of pleasant or memorable activities. I can pick through the lists and decide which ones I want to do."

Another patient talked about how friendships can be especially difficult with advanced disease. *"The past five years has taught me that fighting cancer has required a new openness in regards to relationships. I was naive at the beginning of my journey. I thought that all my friends, at the time, would walk this path with me. Yet I noticed that sometimes I needed new friendships. Some of my friends, though they meant well, could not walk with me."*

Facing our Mortality

Cancer pushes us to think about our mortality. Whether it's the cancer you're dealing with or someone else's, it all touches too close to home. Just like aging, it's an unpleasant topic and it's one that is difficult to talk about. We are all going to die eventually; we all know it, but never imagine we might be the one that transitions prematurely. With a serious cancer diagnosis that is a possibility. People are so uncomfortable with the subject that they rarely talk about death unless something forces them to open that topic.

As a survivor, looking at our impermanence can actually be a blessing. Cancer is one of life's challenges that I'm sure stretches the definition of a blessing. After you clock some time and distance post treatment, you may realize that being face to face with the potential of dying is a blessing. This can be a wakeup call that reminds us that life is not a dress rehearsal as I mentioned before, even if you believe in the hereafter as I do, this is all there is for this body. There are no do over's. All we have is the time ahead of us and no one knows if that will be measured in days, years or decades.

I met a woman who loved her job, flying to wonderful places. She was literally gone from her home all but a handful of days a month. Even in the first phase of her treatment, she appreciated that the last six years of jet setting had been exciting and fun, but her grandkids were growing up without her, and that must change for her to be truly in line with her values and priorities.

Talking to the Kids About Advanced Cancer

Kathy laments, *"I never knew how hard cancer was on my family. I thought I was the only one in pain. It was pretty traumatic for my 11 yr. old. She's slowly recovering from the shock, but it's taking time."* No one can describe the feeling that comes over you when your doctor tells you, you have cancer, but even worse, how do you tell your children that same news especially if it is advanced?

Psychologists agree in general it's better to tell the kids rather than withhold important information. Telling your children about a serious cancer diagnosis can be very difficult but it's essential that you think through what you're going to say. The words and the emotions around the words will have a significant impact on how the children will react. The calmer you are, the less frightened they will be; this goes for all ages. Our adult children may experience more trauma as they understand the potential loss more fully. Encourage them to seek professional guidance if they are struggling to find the words. Also, remember the power of nonverbal communication and try to match your words and your body language.

Kids and adolescents require an approach based on their age and coping skills. However, talking about cancer is essential for children of all ages. In doing so, they learn that their families are there for assistance and they can count on their families to be honest with them. Give them time to grasp the information and an opportunity to ask questions.

Even youngsters should be encouraged to talk about their feelings. Help them to express their feelings and reassure them of your love. It is easiest for children to show their feelings using activities such as puppets, or painting or coloring; older children might prefer writing poetry or drawing. There may be meetings available for children and adult children to process their feelings around cancer and your treatment of the disease.

Cancer Affects Kids No Matter What Age

Children of all ages will have a variety of reactions to the news of their parent having cancer. Some young people are worriers, some are very sensitive to the fear and anxiety of the parents, and some seem not to be affected. Most want to know the details and how they can fix this problem, but, this one can't be fixed by them. They can sense a parent's anxiety and fear so keep the communications open and allow them to help when and where they can. This may be an opportunity to spend quality time with your grown children that has eluded you for years because of proximity or busyness of life. I read a good book by Will Schwalbe called *"The End of Your Life Book Club"* where Will's mom was diagnosed with pancreatic cancer. He used their common love of books to spend precious time together and talk about difficult topics that mattered while describing his perspective of the journey. He used books to relate to his mom and what she was experiencing, to process his grief and to understand what was truly important.

You Can Thrive

I had a delightful conversation with a very young patient who had just gotten the news that the cancer had gone to her brain and the drugs weren't working. She was only 36 when she got this overwhelming news. As we sat having coffee at a local coffee shop she told me that she had actually been given the gift of wisdom. I remember looking at her with a puzzled look and she explained that most people at her age don't have the opportunity to see life through the lens she had. Most are much older and have lived and experienced so much more than she had at her age. She felt blessed to have been given the chance to receive the wisdom of knowing what was really important and be able talk to those most crucial in her life about these things. I walked away from that coffee date thinking she was wise beyond her years and what a gift she had given me by sharing her insights. She saw cancer as a gift. I know that's a stretch for most of us, but life seems to work this way sometimes. So ask yourself, what do I want to learn or understand from this experience? What is the wakeup call I want or even need to learn from this journey? This thought process might be tough for some however I think it is worth at least spending some time contemplating.

Evelyn reminded me that even though she has metastatic disease it doesn't have to define her. *"There are so many free services that are available for support that you just need to start asking and learn to become your own advocate. You must be proactive. Don't give in to depression. Get up, get ready for the day and have goals to achieve for yourself and others. Make more plans for tomorrow."*

Treatment Isn't Working, So Now What?

One positive aspect from a cancer diagnosis is, most people even with the absolute worse news have some time. Cancer rarely takes us so quickly that we don't have the chance to take care of personal business and relationships. The way I explain it, there are much worse ways of dying. If you receive this kind of disappointing news, in spite of everything you usually have time to accomplish many things that will make your passing easier. If you must hear those fateful words, "the treatment isn't working and there nothing more we can do except make you comfortable," there usually are opportunities to do the important things.

It's never easy to lose someone we care about, but at least with cancer, people generally have time to say the things that need to be said. Some people aren't demonstrative with their feelings and don't express their love well verbally. This may be the only time they feel comfortable enough to get out what they have held back for years. We can apologize for the things we did or didn't do, talk about regrets and be able to leave this earth with a lighter heart. We have time to talk about the will, who inherits what, and why, so there aren't any surprises down the road.

Process this information and live your life. Figure out the details if you haven't done that yet, document your wishes and live the rest of your life without regrets, whatever time you have left. None of us look forward to this chapter of our lives, but if you are exhausted and can't go on any longer, it's understandable. Let go when the time comes, it's alright not to fight any more.

Facing these details can be daunting but medical directives are simply a list of questions to take the guesswork out of the process and get your desires met when the time comes. Think about the way you want to die. Do you want to be resuscitated or not? Make these decisions when emotions are not so high. Place that information where loved ones know where it is, in the home, safety deposit box and with your doctor and hospital. When the time comes they will follow your instructions. You take the burden off of your family to make these emotionally charged decisions. Whether you make your wishes known in a will, living trust, advanced directive or another vehicle, your wishes are important. Make them known and then stop worrying about dying and <u>LIVE</u>.

To make this easier, my husband and I have created a "Simple Estate Organizer" to help you capture all of your important information in one place to ease this process. This book it can be ordered on Amazon as well.

I had one sweet lady goes so far as to write her eulogy and pick out all the songs for her celebration of life. She told me the only thing left is to put the picture board together, that way she can pick the pictures and memories she wants to share. Talk about the ultimate control.

We have control over so little in reality. We have control over how we think, how we behave and how we project ourselves. We have no control how others perceive us, how others react to our behaviors and actions. We can't change even a moment of the past and we can't control the future. All we have is the here and now. Our thoughts, our choices, and our behaviors.

Leslie explained, *"Cancer forced me to face my own mortality and deal with the very real possibility that I may not live into my 80's, as most of my grandparents did, as well as my parents, who are still living. I've changed my lifestyle in terms of diet, exercise, etc. and cut back my job responsibilities and hours worked. I also try to approach each day with a different perspective than I had previously (less stress and worrying, more "let it go, don't sweat the small stuff" and more living in the moment), and appreciate things large and small a little bit more. I'm also being a little more spontaneous and doing things that previously I may have analyzed more before deciding to do. I try to constantly remind myself that no one knows how long they have on the planet so make the most of the time you have."*

Time is precious for all of us but so often we take it for granted. Faced with our demise we take the time and energy to think about our wishes. When I have these hard conversations with a woman about transitioning, we talk about how she wants to be remembered. This is a great opportunity to pull out the old pictures, create a photo book or album that captures those memories. One suggestion is to audio or video record your memories and accounts about people that are special to you. Tell the stories that bring you and others joy and happiness. Friends and family will remember you after you are gone. Your memories will be buried with you unless you share them with others or at least write them down to be shared later.

I was blessed to be a part of one woman's legacy. She wanted to thank everyone in her life who had played a part in her care, her inspiration, and her life. She, with the assistance of another friend, recorded the stories; the words she wanted to make sure were delivered to those she loved deeply. My friend carefully categorized the photos and words. She asked great questions to capture the spirit of the message she wanted to convey. I arranged the photos and matched up the messages to create a finished photobook. The book showcased each of these special people, their dying friend's thoughts, and her feelings of gratitude in the last few weeks of her life. The timing was incredible. The books were delivered to her the day before she died. With the help of her husband, she was able to see the pictures and listen to her own words so artfully crafted to those that meant the most to her in the world. The gift was then delivered to those people at her memorial and will be part of her legacy forever.

Death with Dignity

Death with Dignity is an interesting concept. Death with Dignity is an end-of-life option that allows a qualified person to legally request and obtain medications from their physician to end their life in a peaceful, humane, and dignified manner at a time and place of their choosing. To qualify under Death with Dignity laws, you must be an adult resident of a state where a Death with Dignity law is in effect (OR, WA, VT presently); mentally competent, i.e. capable of making and communicating your healthcare decisions; diagnosed with a terminal illness that will lead to death within six months, as confirmed by two physicians. The process entails two oral requests, one written request, waiting periods, and other requirements.[27] It's not an inexpensive alternative, the drugs are close to $3000 and they aren't covered by any insurance plan.

I live in Oregon and it is one of the states where it is legal to choose the time of your death when enduring a disease like cancer. In Oregon, reports show that up to 97% of people using Oregon's Death with Dignity law are on hospice at the time of death and 69% have cancer. Oregon has some of the best pain, palliative and hospice care in the nation. The laws encourages physicians to better diagnose depression, need for pain management, and hospice referrals.

---

[27] https://www.deathwithdignity.org/faqs/

Part 3

Chapter 9

Moving Toward Your Best Self

What does moving forward mean after you just finished cancer treatment? The doctors say I'm cured but I don't feel confident of that or that cancer won't come back. You join millions of cancer survivors that feel the same way. The reality is, we have no guarantees none of us, cancer survivor or not. Before our cancer we didn't think about it, or dwell on it like we do now. We were busy living our lives, not thinking about our mortality, but now that you have finished cancer treatment, things are different. Or, are they really?

Don't Die Before You Die

Living is a choice. As long as you are breathing, you have that choice. I talked about my adopted mother in the beginning of this book and how she lived to the age of 76. She was cremated and her ashes were put into an urn but she really died many years before. Her spirit was crushed and she existed in a lonely shell she had created. I have only a few memories of her happy or really living and that is a crime. We all know people like this and I find it very sad especially when others I know are fighting for all they have to live a few more days or months.

Choose life for as long as you can, choose to laugh, learn, explore and be all you can be. We all have days, even seasons that are troubled and tumultuous, but there are moments even in those worst of times that are worth savoring. Don't die before it's your time.

Can't Change the Past

Carol recalls *"I cannot emphasize enough how much we all need to relearn how to live after we have come face to face with a major health crisis that can potentially rob you of all the life you have left to live. Now, I just live one day at a time and enjoy that day."*

You had cancer, or in some cases you may continue to have cancer. As much as the doctors would love to have a magic wand to fix that, they can't. So come to grips with that fact. Understand we can't go back. It wasn't fair that you got cancer and someone else didn't, but for your emotional health, taking steps toward acceptance is necessary.

Again, don't waste the time you have lamenting how unfair it is or fighting the treatment process. Enjoy each day you are given on this earth and be a blessing for those around you. Cancer can remind us in a not so gentle manner that our time is measured and how sacred it is. Choose not to take that for granted. Use the time you are given for the betterment of your world and not on worrying about the past or things beyond your control.

Manage Your Expectations

My husband and I went camping one Labor Day weekend several years ago. I remember it was near a tiny little community near the coast in Oregon. I had no idea what to expect, other than that we were going camping to relax and enjoy the long weekend together. We didn't have a schedule so we were open to what came our way. We set up our camp only steps from the Umpqua River and were excited to see if we could catch some fish. Fishing was amazing; every time we put our hooks in the water within a couple of minutes we were pulling another one out. They weren't large but they were plentiful. I can remember my husband literally pulling me off the bank because the sun had gone down and I was begging to hook just one more. I bet we caught over 200 fish between the two of us. We released all but a few, enough to cook up over the fire that night. It was like a dream for anyone who enjoys fishing, which I now know is different from "catching!" The next day was the same; we were in heaven being in such a beautiful place, peaceful and serene while pulling in fish after fish for hours.

Along with our fishing we did a little exploring and found that on Labor Day there would be a butterfly release near a beautiful garden. Taking nature photographs is one of my hobbies and I especially love taking photos of flowers and butterflies, so I was thrilled. The mysterious part was that because the butterflies were kept in a structure for several days before being released they learn they can't go anywhere so they stay in a small area for a day or two after being released. When they are let out of their enclosure they hang out in the garden for about 24 to 48 hours not realizing they can go any further. I was ready with my camera as the release happened and took some amazing photos of monarch butterflies perched on colorful zinnias for what seemed like hours. I couldn't get enough, just like the fishing. I walked away completely satiated from my fishing and photography that weekend.

When spring and summer came the following year I was very enthusiastic about going back to the same campground and experiencing the same level of excitement over the fishing and the opportunity to photograph my favor subjects. That weekend camping trip was when I learned a valuable lesson. We camped in almost the same spot on the same weekend, went to the same place in the river to fish, and went to the same butterfly release on Labor Day. With great anticipation we hit the river with our same poles, gear and bait. We fished for two days and struggled to catch enough fish for one meal. The water was much warmer than it had been the year before so the moss was thick. Instead of reeling in fish after fish, our lines got tangled and clogged with moss and sticks. On Labor Day, anticipating my coveted photographic opportunity, we found the garden in complete disrepair, dried up with only a couple of blooms. It was as if it had gone all year without any attention. Needless to say the butterflies found no reason to hang out and dissipated quickly without posing for me.

I was disappointed and lamented returning to this sleepy little community on the Oregon coast to try to relive the previous year's spectacular adventure. Although it didn't measure up to the previous year, I found myself looking for new memories and experiences that would make that long weekend memorable in other ways. We can't recreate and relive the past. I learned that trip how important it is to be open to new experiences and not try to recreate old ones. We need to be grateful for past adventures but it's a waste of time and energy to depend on the past for today's happiness. This goes for holidays as well, like Christmas. It doesn't have to be done all in one day. Whether it's a birthday, Thanksgiving or Christmas, it doesn't have to be celebrated the same way others do. Make it work for you to be meaningful and memorable. Take the time you need to enjoy the experience. When we have so many expectations of what the perfect holiday or event looks like, we are setting ourselves up for failure and disappointment. We will miss new opportunities and be frustrated, besides. Embrace the here and now, not what used to be, or what could or should have been.

Moving On

Everyone is different in how we process this crazy journey but there are similarities that run very deep. Cheri explains it like this, *"For me, I was not prepared for all that would be asked of me to complete my treatment. There were procedures in the beginning that seemed to move so quickly it made my head spin. I had never been sick, so I didn't have a point of reference to surgery and the healing process. I did not feel comfortable taking any medicine. Cancer took over my life. It affected my mind, body and spirit. I found support and moved through the treatment and had a planned schedule. What I discovered after I completed treatment was that I was not the same person. I had changed. I no longer wanted to participate in life's drama. The folks that were caring for me during treatment were now my family. Some family members really let me down and there was grief associated with those feelings. I felt like I was dismissed from treatment and had to start over. I was still traumatized and did not have adequate energy for months after radiation. The new normal has been a whole new journey. Life is more precious and I know that I live more consciously now. My circle of people has changed. My work changed. I can honestly say that every aspect of my world is different. Yes, coming out of the cancer experience was a huge wake up call to treasure life and the time that we are here."*

Linda found her re-entry to life after treatment challenging. *"My cancer journey was a life-changing experience. I quickly realized how difficult it was to re-enter the world of reality which included grocery shopping and working at the office. I learned this the hard way by going to the grocery store, being frightened of all the people around me, freezing with my hands on the cart, starting to cry. I quickly abandoned my cart containing the items I had selected to purchase and walked as fast as I could to the shelter of my automobile sitting in the parking lot. It takes time to rethink and reorganize one's priorities after a journey through cancer land. There is great benefit to preparing one's emotional state for re-entering the world of reality."* Like Linda and Cheri, we all have a story about the moment we come to the realization our lives have been impacted in a way that's hard to explain to anyone who hasn't been there. This is where our lives as we knew them don't exist. Some are dramatic like these two stories and some much more subtle but we are all affected in ways that change the way we see life and the future.

Kathy describes her journey, *"I look back at the stages I went through, kind of like chapters in a book. There was a time when the support group was needed. The ladies at my church prayed for me, my visit to Breast Friends was helpful for compassion and to get more resources. All these people were so vital for my ability to move on."* As Kathy mentions, it is a process. There is no specific order that is right or wrong, but we need to spend time in the different stages or chapters to come out the other side a better more enlightened person. The hard part is we have to do it ourselves. No one can accomplish this for us. They can walk through it with us, but they can't replace us in this journey.

Janet said, *"It has been a year since my last radiation treatment. It's hard to believe all that happened last year and now here I am back to work, back to normal and feeling absolutely wonderful. However, it is always in the back of my mind wondering if and when the cancer will return. Will it be soon? How will I know? How do I prepare if it is? How long will I have? So right now I am trying to figure out how to deal with and minimize those thoughts."*

As Janet mentions, she's doing great but ultimately must deal with that nagging feeling in the back of her head about cancer. She has moved on but understands what she has control over and that is the positive attitude she takes into each day.

There are actual health benefits of optimism and positive thinking. Researchers at the Mayo Clinic[28] continue to explore the aspects of positive thinking and optimism on health. Health benefits that positive thinking may provide include:

- Increased life span
- Lower rates of depression
- Lower levels of distress
- Greater resistance to the common cold
- Better psychological and physical well-being
- Reduced risk of death from cardiovascular disease
- Better coping skills during hardships and times of stress

It's unclear why people who engage in positive thinking experience these health benefits. One theory is that having a positive outlook enables you to cope better with stressful situations, which reduces the harmful health effects of this pressure on your body.

Celebrate the Little Things

We are the luckiest, richest people in the world, even if you aren't feeling that way right now. Compared to the rest of the world we who live in the United States are blessed. Most of us have clean drinking water, food to eat, a place to sleep, clothes to wear and clean air to breathe.

---

[28] http://www.mayoclinic.com/health/positive-thinking/SR00009

Sometimes we forget to be thankful and celebrate these things. We spend so much time thinking and talking about all the things we want or need, what we don't have and what we are lacking we forget to assess and appreciate the things we have. I'm going to take it one step further; I would love to have you get into the habit of not only appreciating these little things but celebrating them.

Think of the things we take for granted like normal bodily functions, clean drinking water, and food in our refrigerators and pantries. Make it a habit to think about how you live and the good fortune you have, even if you are struggling. You are richer than 98% of the world.

Glenna shared her perspective on how hope is another way to talk about positive outlook or optimism. *"I have found hope is foundational to facing all cancers but especially stage IV cancer. At all cost, no matter what, I must keep hope alive; if I am going to keep me alive. I have collected a variety of hope refreshing actions that I can do on a daily bases. I use as many approaches as I can, prayer, meditation, supportive friends, reading of other people's healing journey, writing out affirmations and Scripture. I walk through lush parks, breath in the fresh morning air, putter with flowers; anything that will nurture hope or distract my mind from moving toward despair."*

This patient understands what she needs to keep a positive attitude. It takes balance to make course corrections. With advanced disease she can reflect how she dealt with the original cancer and how she deals with more advanced disease. She chooses to look for the positive, rather than dwell on the negative. She has tough moments, tough hours and even some tough days, but embraces those as normal. She then moves past those negative feelings to joy, gratitude, happiness and her optimistic outlook.

Write a Gratitude Journal

Appreciating what we have may take practice. Sometimes we can get into a habit of complaining or taking things for granted. Especially when life throws us a curve ball, we can feel sorry for ourselves and forget how many wonderful things continue to be present in our life. Taking the time to remind ourselves of the wonderful things is a good practice to add to your day.

Some women find it helpful to journal their thankfulness. I know some days it's more difficult to find things to be grateful for, but if you start by merely writing little things down, it helps. Some things you write may sound ridiculous but write them down. Start out with little things like *'I'm thankful I got out of bed today, or I'm thankful I have food in my refrigerator.'* That's actually not a little thing as some can't say they can get out of bed nor had food in their refrigerator. We take so much for granted. We can walk and talk and have the freedom to go to the store, have money to spend when we get there and have a cool place to store the food when we get home.

Find a journal or a notebook with blank pages. Start creating a list of the things you are thankful for. Write at least a few new things each day and re-read the ones you have written before. Within a short time you will notice a difference in your attitude. If you don't feel like writing, cut out fun colors or images that represent gratitude and the feelings you are dealing with. A thankful box, cards, images, shells, rocks whatever reminds you of that person or the feeling you want to reproduce. No matter how you do this exercise you will create a renewed appreciation for what you have and realize we all have struggles but we have so much to be grateful for.

Here are some examples, there is no right way, or wrong way. Just have fun with it, be sincere and dig deep.

List three things I am grateful for today.

When you begin or if you've had a tough day perhaps it will look like this:
Jan 1, 2018
1. I'm grateful I didn't get a hangover from the party last night
2. I'm grateful I could get out of bed
3. I'm grateful I don't have to apologize for my behaviors last night since I didn't get drunk

List three things I am grateful for today.

With a little practice and on better days, it might look like this:

March 1, 2018
1. I'm grateful for my supportive talented husband
2. I'm grateful for the clouds and the blue sky
3. I'm grateful for the conversation I had with my daughter

Forgiveness

Even though we know we can't go back and change anything in the past, I think we all hold on to the fantasy that we can. If we worry and fret over what was, it seems like it should have some impact, right? But unfortunately it doesn't change a moment of the past. Let go of things in the past. Forgive yourself for missteps, lost opportunities or things that bring up guilt or shame from the past. Holding on isn't going to make them go away or change the outcome of these memories. There are ways to counteract mistakes or hurtful things you've done. Start with an apology, make amends and then let it go and move on.

We all have a few things we regret or we wish were different. No matter how much energy we put into that kind of thinking we can't change those facts. I love this great saying by Elisha Goldstein, Ph.D., *"Forgiveness means giving up all hope for a better past."* Forgive yourself and others. Ask those in your life to forgive you for your part in that disagreement. Put a different spin on those negative thoughts so they can actually be positive. Decide what's most important, being right, or the relationship? Perhaps the cancer has caused chaos in your life, so look at what has come out of this experience from a positive perspective. It will help you be gentle on yourself and others, forgiving in the process. It is a more productive way to move forward from the cancer.

When others hurt us, it's important to process those feelings as well. Forgiveness isn't to help those who have hurt us, it's for us. Bishop T.D. Jakes said it well, *"Unforgiveness is like drinking poison and waiting for the other person to die."*

I remember hearing a story about a woman who was so mad at an old friend from high school that even 20 years later she was still fretted about it. Every time she thought about the incident it made her furious. When she finally brought up the incident to her old friend at the 20 year reunion, her friend didn't even remember the incident. The old friend could tell it was continuing to upset her, so she apologized sincerely for the past behavior even though she didn't recall the day in question.

I think of this often when I feel violated or hurt in a way that I feel justifies holding on to a grudge. Reminding myself of this story, I ask, what good does it do to hold onto those bad feelings? Think about those unresolved situations in your life and figure out what needs to happen to let them go. If you are mad at your father and he's been gone for 10 years, who is that hurting? If you have a friend that betrayed you, find them and have a conversation. Ask them to forgive you for your part of the problem, tell them you have forgiven them. Offer the apology to someone you have hurt. Then let those hurts go, forgive and move on. Remember, forgiving is not forgetting. I'm not asking you to be best buds with someone who has hurt you, but I am suggesting you forgive them for your sake.

Spirituality is Different for Everyone

Spirituality is different for everyone. Some of us have gravitated toward organized religion from our childhood, the roots we grew up with and understand. Others find organized religion difficult to relate to and need to find their spirituality elsewhere. This may be in a building, in nature, or in a special corner at home. The place isn't as important as the time you spend exploring what it all means. Some find it helpful to bounce around from one tradition to another. Experience a Jewish prayer shawl even if you aren't Jewish. Use a Rosary to remember the good things in your life or affirmations, even if you aren't Catholic. Light some candles and use them to focus. Whatever works for you!

I used my faith in God to bolster my spirits in those tough times. Moments when things felt dark and bleak, my beliefs were renewed and my spirit restored when I remembered to lean on God.

God gives us all special strengths and talents and I believe we all have a purpose on this earth. Some talents and gifts are so obvious we take them for granted. I remember many years ago I took an online strengths test. It took over an hour to complete and when it tabulated my results I was excited to be wowed with the findings. I expected to unveil something amazing.

My number one strength is positivity and the funny thing was, that made me angry. I was completely irritated that I had spent over an hour completing this test for it to tell me I was Mary Sunshine. I knew that. The fact that I am happy most of the time. I can find something good even in a terrible situation. What was I going to do with the gift of positivity?

Well, come to find out, I do Breast Friends. I work with cancer patients and give them hope when they are feeling hopeless. I have the natural ability to turn a woman from crying and in emotional distress to laughing and joking around. That's how I use my natural strength of positivity.

Some strengths are less obvious, but the world sees them. Some are hidden until the right doors are opened; none are more valuable than the next. These very personal gifts have been given to all of us. Some are meant to be shown, some are meant to be taught, and some are meant to pass on to others. We all have these special qualities; the trick is to recognize those gifts, strengths and talents and figure how best to use them. It would be a shame not to use these natural abilities to do what God put you on this earth to do.

Jan remembers "A month before I was diagnosed I embarked on a health program and lost a significant amount of weight. The diagnosis gave me an added incentive to follow through with my goals. The courage required to complete testing and surgery helped me gain self-confidence and self-respect. I realized that I needed to address feelings of grief surrounding the death of my father and I turned to my faith for the support to move forward. I look at cancer as a wakeup call. I was fortunate that it was found early, and I want to use the experience to create a more purposeful life."

With several years to reflect on my breast cancer journey and my involvement in Breast Friends, I understand I've had a wonderful opportunity to discover my purpose and use my strengths. Most of us go through life and don't understand why we are on this earth. We don't understand our worth, our strengths or what we should do with them.

Our society seems to concentrate mostly on our weaknesses and working to improve those rather than playing up our strengths. I have been able to put my assets to work to help others deal with their breast cancer. I wake up each day knowing in my heart I am doing the right things for the right reasons. I am still learning, I still struggle with lack of confidence, but I know in my heart my involvement in Breast Friends is making a difference.

Connecting your strengths and talents with those things you are passionate about will allow you to find your purpose, then use those talents to fuel your passion. Here's a guide to help you get closer to understanding both your strengths and your passion.

Passion

Principles- Our core values that differentiate you from me.
Attitudes- The way you think about yourself and others.
Strengths- The things you are naturally good at and enjoy.
Skills- Those abilities you've been able to learn.
Identity- Roles we play and what they mean to us.
Opportunities- The growth prospects we are faced with.
New Life- Combining passion with strengths for happier future. [29]

Take Time to Be Quiet and Think

In our crazy busy over-stimulated society, we barely have the time, or more likely we don't take the time to sit in a quiet room for any length of time and think. For years I was one to always have the TV on for background noise, but was that actually true? Was I trying to block out the

---

[29] Appendix 4 Passion

small quiet voice? The quiet can be almost deafening. I have to admit it took some getting used to the quiet. Being motionless and quiet can be a daunting task. I know people that are never not moving or silent. The thought of being calm and still seems very frightening. It takes repetition, so as I write this book I practice. I find a few moments each day where I consciously find my quiet place and sit motionless. Let go of your agenda, let the stillness simply be. Start off with a couple of minutes and practice being quiet and motionless. Then add a few minutes at a time.

Being busy is a habit just like all the other things we do. I was in a habit of not thinking and not listening to my inner voice. I have found a new way to be okay with the silence and it's actually quite refreshing. It feels uncomfortable at first, but so do most things when we are changing our habits.

When I practice being still, emotions often well up. I'm not always sure where they come from but my instinct is to get up and get busy so I don't feel those emotions. My mind races at first. So many thoughts and feelings all colliding that it catches me off-guard. Gradually, my thoughts begin to slow down and become clearer. It's like walking into a room full of chaos with many different conversations going on at the same time. One faction talks louder than the rest to be heard, then another. The volume increases as I stand and watch. Standing there quietly a few people notice my presence, finish up their conversations and turn their attention to me. Slowly the volume comes down and more and more attention is on me. Pretty soon I have the floor. That's what being quiet feels like to me. It takes a while to get all the thoughts and conversations in my head to slow down and pay attention to only one. God needs this stillness, this quiet, so we can hear his voice within us and know what direction to take. He wants to show us how to deal with the pressures of life, to heal our bodies and our souls during and after our cancer journey.

Spend time with God or your higher power by being still and listening. You will find clarity in your life. Don't get caught up on how you hear the voice. I have never heard an audible voice; perhaps some do. It can come to you in a thought, especially one you haven't had before. It can come in an intuition, a feeling, or a dream. I had a feeling of terrible foreboding one weekend I couldn't shake until I did something about it. I acted on this feeling and then it subsided. Don't give up if you don't have an earth-shattering epiphany and the earth doesn't tremble under your chair. Be quiet enough to hear the whisper when it comes, and it will come.

Slowing down enough to think in the hustle-bustle of life seems like an impossible task. It feels very self-indulgent and selfish when there are dishes in the sink, errands to run and no time for some of the other things we need to do. Maybe that's part of what we need to think about. What is it I truly want to spend my time on? And how does that relate to the big picture of what I am meant or designed to do in this life?

Listening to your inner voice is considered by many as a way of communicating with your higher power. Some consider the inner voice to be our conscience. That voice in our head tells us something doesn't feel right, or a special awareness that we can't always explain. This can be a dialogue that asks questions and searches for answers. Whatever you believe, we can all benefit from the practice of being quiet and listening. Be still and listen to this inner voice. Sometimes it whispers and sometimes it shouts. It's easy to ignore, especially when you aren't still enough to hear those whispers. Even the shouts can be drowned out by using enough mind altering substances like drugs or alcohol to numb the pain and discomfort of life.

Take some time and learn how to listen to your inner voice. It takes some work and doesn't come automatically, it takes practice. With time and practice you will come to know and trust that voice. You will find the answers that are right for you within you. You have the inner wisdom to know what is best, if you take the time and energy to ask yourself the important questions and listen quietly for the answers. You have the opportunity, while you are listening, to access and assess what you want and need in your life. This isn't a time to beat yourself up for all the things you haven't done or the opportunities you have missed. Don't go back and relive those moments. Learn from them and find ways to not repeat those experiences. Choose to reject those negative thoughts and replace them with more productive ones.

Elizabeth asked her doctor, *"When I finished my treatment, I asked my medical oncologist, 'What happens now?' She said, 'now, it's a question of faith and time.' At the time, I thought it was a tad simplistic but I decided to embrace the 'faith' part as my way of dealing with the 'time' part. Literally, I meditate. And when I do, I visualize my body and spirit as perfect and my body as cancer free. I hold that vision as the only reality for me. We must enjoy each day and the way I do that is through gratitude for each day and each day's health"*

I tend to be on the treadmill of life like many of you. I get up each morning and do what I did yesterday out of habit. It's easy. I don't have to think about it. But is that the best way to live my life? After a cancer experience it seems only fitting and proper to actually get off this treadmill and figure out what we were put on this earth to do. If, after some time and reflection you decide the life you are living is the one you want, then bravo for you. Go live that life and enjoy the rest of it in joy. No regrets. However, if you can imagine the end and have regrets, now is the time to redirect that path.

I find my time in nature allows me to be thoughtful, to be filled with appreciation and awe for the beauty all around me. I use my photography to capture and enjoy those moments and also to look back on and remember for years to come. I enjoy roaming around and seeking out the beauty, listening to the birds chattering to one another. I enjoy the smells and the feeling of being part of something much bigger.

Many find reading or listening to motivational material helpful. Sometimes, when life is doing all the talking and I need stillness, plugging into an audio book while I am driving is like medicine to my soul. I can listen to my favorite author remind me of the things I know I have forgotten, or have gotten so busy I don't take the time to do. I remember reading, *29 Gifts* by Cami Walker the first time and found it was a great reminder of gratitude. I recommend it often to the women I coach. Find an author you click with and devour what they have to say. Read and re-read and try on their practices that might work for you.

I also find that God places people in my life when I need them. Sometimes it appears that I am the one helping them, but with closer inspection I realize I was the one that needed the assistance. I needed to be reminded of a lesson or a topic I am dealing with. The words come out of my mouth to help someone else and they resonate in my head. I regularly think to myself, that's a good idea for me, or I needed to hear that, and just laugh to myself.

There's No 1-2-3 to Happiness

What is happiness other than an illusion? Happiness is different for everyone. If I asked a room full of people what they meant when they say, I just want to be happy, I would get a room full of different answers. Being happy is subjective and no one else can define that for you. For one person it may be sitting alone in their comfy chair reading a book that takes them into their imagination. For another it could be a room full of people where conversations are buzzing and they are the center of them all. I think being happy is getting in touch with the authentic you. When you are in touch with the real you, you can search out situations that regularly make you feel good, perhaps even twinkle. Knowing what is important to you, what you value and the ability to articulate those needs, will allow you to find happiness.

To know what will make you happy, you need to look for what lights you up from the inside. What gets you excited to talk about, or to experience. When does your volume go up? When do you get animated when you talk, using your hands and gestures more boldly than usual? What makes you twinkle? Not your mom, not your boss, not your partner, but you. Often, we don't even know.

What lights me up are those little things in life that usually don't cost a thing. They sometimes even sneak up on me and, if I'm not careful, I can miss them. It can be in the woods and I see a butterfly that seems to slow down long enough for me to get a good look. Rarely long enough to get a photo, but at least a good look. It can be seeing someone's face light up as we talk, knowing I had something to do with the change in demeanor. It's being a part of something that is bigger than me, that I can contribute my gifts to and make things even better for myself and others.

Take a few minutes and write. Reflect on those little things that can make a smile break out on your face. Write down what made you laugh this week. Remember the times in your life when things were going well, when you were happy. Think about what made that time special. How can you recreate those elements in your life now? You can't go back and relive those times, but there are elements that you can bring back into your life that will create those same feelings.

Remember activities that bring you joy. Maybe playing on the coed softball team was so much fun and brought you immense joy. Perhaps your softball days are over; first rethink that, are they really? Perhaps there's a senior league you could join after you do some conditioning or consider doing some coaching. Or, if you consciously decide that your softball days are over, think about the elements of that activity you enjoyed. Was it the competition? What it being on a team? Or was it meeting up for the social time after the game that actually makes you smile? Figure out what part of the activity made you feel good and replicate that in a different sport or activity.

This week, write down what you were doing or what you were talking about when you got louder and more animated. That will give you a glimpse into your twinkle, or at least one of them. Pay attention when you get excited about something. Maybe its politics, maybe its nature, maybe its sports, maybe its food, that makes your heart start to race and gives you lots to talk about.

Do something with that passion. Join a group of like-minded people. I find Meetup.com is a great place to find activities and people who have similar interests as myself. If you don't find a meeting that interests you, start your own group and start moving mountains.

If you light up and gush about your kids and/or your grandkids, make sure they are a huge part of your life. And if they can't be, then find some other kids or grandkids that can. If you love animals, talk about them, show their photos to friends. You need animals in your life. Whether it is helping out at a no-kill shelter, or having more animals yourself, you need animals in your life. That makes you happy.

Choose Happiness

Since happiness means different things to different people, spend your time, energy and resources regularly on the things that make you feel good. Create experiences where you have lasting memories and activities that move you forward. Plan for your happiness, plan to be happy, expect happiness. Find ways to get what you want even if it's abbreviated. For example, if you like to photograph nature but you live in a city like I do, take short trips to a community garden, park or other venue. Get out in the woods or by the water or find a park or a water feature to hear the peaceful melodic rhythm.

A friend talks about her love of the outdoors, but her health keeps her from going too far away from home, so she will spend an afternoon at the local nursery, enjoying the plants. Think out of the box, you might find you also like taking photos of architectural elements or urban decay so try something you love with a new twist. Explore what you love and look at it from different perspectives. This may open up new avenues you hadn't experienced or even considered.

Invest your time and money in things that are meaningful to you. Many find that spending time with their family creating strong emotional ties brings them happiness. Studies have shown that having strong ties are associated with lower rates of depression, suicide and stress and may even help you live longer. So, create family rituals, game night, dinners or annual family vacations to stay connected.

"Happiness is an emotion, a feeling. Optimism is a belief about the future," says Suzanne Segerstrom, Ph.D., a professor of psychology at the University of Kentucky. *"Optimism enhances well-being because it leads to greater engagement with life."*[30]

Optimism is a choice. I have coined an acronym for H.O.P.E as Healthy Optimism, Positive Energy. To me Healthy Optimism is the feeling that despite frustrations or something bad happening, things will turn out well in the

---

[30] http://www.redbookmag.com/body/mental-health/how-to/a4845/be-an-optimist/

end. In spite of our best efforts we may have a bad outcome, but the journey will be better and more enjoyable with this Health Optimism and ultimately hope. Positive Energy is the sunshine you carry in your heart, the positive feeling that puts a smile on your face even on a rainy day. It is the personal power you choose to bring into the world, even when it feels so much bigger than little old me. That is what hope looks like to me. It may sound a little Polly Annish, but sometimes the feeling of hope doesn't make logical sense. It just is.

So why do we struggle with hope? What makes one person hopeful and another negative? Unfortunately there are no simple answers to these questions. For some it is something that we must work at constantly. I do believe the way we see ourselves and what we believe we deserve does have an enormous impact on hope. So, let's talk about ways we can improve our self-esteem and then we will improve our ability to feel hopeful.

Create a Positive Mindset

I am a positive person with a sunny disposition by nature, and based on the experts and the studies they have performed, that positive attitude should keep me alive longer. Breast cancer survivors who initially adopted a fighting spirit live longer than those responding with fatalism and hopelessness. (Even the distress level of the breast cancer patient's partner significantly affects the distress level of the patient can affect her quality and length of her life.)

We all know that person who seems to have a black cloud following them around. If something bad is going to happen, it's going to happen to them. We can create this environment with our own self-talk. Between negative self-esteem, negative self-talk and a negative belief system we can literally create blindness to positive opportunities. In

196

contrast, expecting positive experiences creates positive outcomes. Shawn Achor describes an experiment by Dr. Richard Wiseman in his book, The Happiness Advantage, which proves this. Dr. Wiseman was trying to demonstrate why some people seem to be consistently lucky while others can't catch a break. It turned out that the difference is whether you expect good things or bad things to happen. Either way, you're probably right. If you think you are lucky you'll be luckier. Let me explain. Dr. Wiseman asked volunteers to read through a newspaper and count the ads. The lucky ones, who thought they were generally lucky, took a few seconds to complete the task while the unlucky ones took a full two minutes. Why was there such a big difference? On the second page of the newspaper there was a very large ad that read, "Stop reading, there are 43 ads in this newspaper." It was plain as day, but those who were self-described themselves as unlucky were far more likely to miss it. As an additional bonus, about half way through the newspaper another large ad said, "Stop counting, tell the experimenter you saw this ad and you win $250."[31] The people who believed they were unlucky in life also tended to miss this opportunity. To me, this experiment reinforces the idea that a person with a positive mindset is more likely to see positive opportunities. They are subconsciously searching for opportunities are open to receive the good that comes from them. Those with a negative mindset may be unable to receive and may not even see the opportunities for a better life, or the options to change. If you are open to receiving you will be open to more positive opportunities.

---

[31] https://www.psychologytoday.com/articles/201005/make-your-own-luck

Chapter 10

Impact of Self Esteem and Choices

We live in a time where we are constantly bombarded with images, ideas and sound bites that tell us who we should be, could be and ought to be. The media continuously reminds us we are never thin enough, pretty enough, tall enough, or even young enough. Unless you live under a rock, you can't escape these self-defeating messages every day all pointing to one main message, *'You are not good enough.'*

Then throw a cancer diagnosis and treatment into the mix, add the scars, misshapen breasts from surgery and/or reconstruction, no nipples, no cleavage and what do you have? And don't forget that hair, even though it does grow back, it doesn't come back in the same. Cancer can smash our self-esteem into tiny bits. A once confident person can be riddled with feelings of not feeling good enough. So it's not a surprise that after cancer some of us are crippled emotionally with low self-esteem.

Self-esteem impacts every aspect of our lives and plays a major role in our adaptation of our life after cancer. It can affect our thoughts and feelings about ourselves, whether or not we deserved the cancer, or if we deserve to go on. It can affect our thoughts and beliefs whether or not we believe the cancer will come back. Our sense of self-worth is how we see ourselves (physically, mentally, emotionally, and spiritually), if we are strong and courageous or weak and undeserving. Self-esteem is what we believe to be true about ourselves, our competencies or the lack of abilities seen through our filters rather than reality or what's seen through the eyes of others. Because of these beliefs we can avoid taking chances or avoid going after what we really want. Some of us stick our head in the sand rather than change what we don't like in life or go after what makes us happy.

Our outlook, our attitudes and beliefs affect our employment, our relationships, our friendships, and our overall wellbeing. Low self-esteem hampers our getting into good relationships as well as getting out of bad ones. The filters we use to view others can be distorted and this affects how we relate to the rest of the world. The kind of relationships we attract can be healthy, or not so healthy, depending on the thoughts and feelings we have about ourselves and the lives we believe we deserve. It influences our decisions, choices and our life experiences either positively or negatively. It affects how we live our lives every day and can manifest exactly what we think we deserve.

Self Esteem Assessment

Now let's do an exercise to assess where your self-esteem lies presently. I want you to write down 20 positive phrase or words that best describe you. Don't second guess yourself, just write. If you get stuck before getting all 20 positive words, I want you to ask a few of the people in your life for help to get all 20 words or phrases. Even if you don't agree, write them down without arguing or minimizing what they say.

I'll tell you a secret, the first time I did this exercise I got to six and got stuck. My negative self-talk took over and derailed me from getting past six positive words. I've continued to do this and other exercises and have improved the positive thoughts about myself dramatically. I can now get all twenty words with time to spare. Don't feel bad if you get stuck. If you find yourself struggling ask those in your life who matter to you. The positive opinions of others can remind you what a wonderful person you are. I love it when my ladies ask their kids. The answers are so sweet and honest and should not be dismissed no matter how old the kids. Embrace the positive words others say about you. These people really know and love the real you.

Read your list a few times a day. At least once in the morning and at the end of the day until you own those words and phrases and can repeat this exercise with much more confidence. Then on your low days you have this wonderful list to remind yourself what a fabulous person you actually are.

Positive Affirmations

Your thoughts and words both verbally and self-talk are vital for improving your self-esteem and for personal growth. We sometimes need a little help to remember the good things about ourselves and that's where positive affirmations come into play. Even if you don't feel you are living up to these things all of the time, it's okay. This is where we start building up your self-worth rather than tear it down.

Since we all engage in continuous self-talk about ourselves, other people, and our lives, it is essential to listen to this chatter and modify it when necessary. An average of 80% of our self-talk is negative. This self-talk influences our thinking, feelings, and eventually our behaviors. Too often, a negative voice of a parent or spouse is the one we hear in our self-talk. I call this the committee. The committee are all the people in our lives past and present who seem to have an opinion about who we are and how we should live our lives. These are the voices that influence our lives and they can be positive or negative. Unfortunately, the negative chatter can constantly invade our thoughts and decisions and makes judgements about ourselves and others. We allow this committee to remind us of our faults and mistakes and then relive them over and over again so they are difficult to forget. It's important to be aware of our thoughts and language and purposely reframe the negative conversations and use words from a more positive point of view.

One trick I use when bombarded with these negative thoughts is to simply stop and ask the question, "Is this true?" This simple action can bring awareness of the negative messaging and give you the opportunity to decide whether you want to continue to believe the voices or not. Some of the noise in our heads has been going on for years and until we stop to ask this question we will continue to believe it and allow it to affect our decisions. What are your voices saying to you? Is it true?

When you find the messaging is untrue, the next step is to reframe or reword your thoughts from a more positive perspective. For instance, if your voice says, "I'm so stupid, I should have known better than to trust that person. I always screw up." Obviously you feel there was an error in judgement made again and you are beating yourselves up for this error. First ask yourself, would I talk like this to anyone else? The answer is usually, "No, I would never say that to a friend," so why do we say it to ourselves?

Perhaps you could reframe this thought to say, "I am a very trusting person and I am a good judge of character, next time I will listen and trust my gut when I see or feel any red flags in my relationships." Don't continue to beat yourself up for something you can't change from the past. Learn from your mistake or missteps and find ways to avoid making them in the future. Now let's add the use of affirmations to build a proactive strategy to build yourself up.

Positive affirmations are a powerful way of replacing negative thoughts with positive statements of self-empowerment. With practice affirmations will become easier. Here's guidelines to follow to create positive self-affirmations

1. Present Tense ("I AM")
Take a stance and state your affirmation in the present tense, as if it already exists ("I AM").

2. Positive
State your conversation in a positive way.

3. Personal
Keep it simple, personal, powerful, and realistic for you.

4. Passion
State and rehearse your conversation with passion.

5. Practice
Repeat your affirmation and declaration several times each day with feeling. Practice for a minimum of 21 continuous days. Post the affirmation on a 3 x 5 card.

Examples of Affirmations

6. I am growing, I trust myself, and I am moving forward.
7. I am strong and I am meeting all of my challenges.
8. I am lovable, nurturing, and capable
9. I am reaching my desired goals.
10. I am living a healthy lifestyle and will have life-long health.
11. I am making wise choices for my life, and I will continue to do so.

Our subconscious is powerful but it doesn't know if what you say is true or not. That's why our negative self-talk is so damaging and these reframing of our words can be so beneficial. When you repeat these positive phrases regularly, morning and night, your mind doesn't question whether they are true yet. Like in "The Help," the nanny repeated over and over again to the little girl "You is Kind, You is Smart, You is Important," so she would remember those words even when her parents said otherwise.

Now think of a few words you want to use as your mantra. I matter, I am enough, I am smart, I am beautiful, I am …. These positive words enter into the subconscious. And when your subconscious hears these words repeatedly it believes what is being said. Then the subconscious creates behaviors that prove the beliefs. You will act kind smart and important otherwise it won't match your subconscious. Your thoughts and actions need to be in line for life to be in balance.

Now let's do the exercise.[32]

- Use positive "I Am" phrases to best describe the person you are and **or want to be** and recite these morning and evening for a month. I've started a list, but come up with other phrases that better suit you.
- Don't hesitate to add those to the list as well. Write these positive statements in the present tense, I am, not I want to be, or I should be.
- Rephrase your affirmations as if they are already true.
- Choose qualities you aspire to have or skills you want to possess but don't feel you have mastered these qualities yet.

---

[32] See appendix 2

For instance,
1. I use positive self-talk to affirm myself daily.
2. I set healthy boundaries for myself and model them for my children.
3. I make decisions wisely and willingly accept the consequences.
4. I discipline myself through managing my thoughts, desires, and expectations.
5. I am healthy, fit and cancer free.

Now write your own and commit to reading them a least twice a day. This works if you will do the work.

As women our positive or negative self-esteem and how we talk to ourselves controls how we see the world, ourselves and how we move forward after cancer. Our self-talk influences us if we see ourselves as victims of cancer, survivors, fighters or thrivers. Instead listen to that little voice inside, whether you say it's your conscience, intuition or the voice of God. Listen to your gut. Be observant of the images you see, feelings you have, and the words you hear. The world teaches us lessons from everything around us and it is important to pay attention so we don't miss the clues. This also means being quiet at times, removing yourself from the chaos of the day and taking time to reflect and listen.

Every person, including you, was born with a set of unique gifts and talents. These are activities or skills that you naturally excel doing. Think about the things that are easy for you, or things that don't take a lot of effort that maybe friends struggle with. These are usually some of those gifts. Many of these traits, strengths and talents are those we take for granted. Many women don't appreciate their own talents because they say it's just who I am. Many of us don't understand how best to use these gifts. Glenna told me *"I know I am creative and if I don't do anything that taps into that creativity I find myself depressed within a couple months."*

Make a list of your gifts and put time and energy toward them every day. Again, like the last exercise, if you are having trouble with your gifts simply ask people in your life you trust. What skills or activities are you naturally good? See what a difference it will make in the way you feel about yourself. This is one way to improve your self-esteem and make for a happier life.

Giving and Receiving

I've noticed that women, while great at giving to others, in truth need practice at receiving. We are generally very self-sufficient, a wonderful ability until it impedes from needing others. During a crisis women rarely ask for help and often end up suffering in silence when friends and family would love to be able to lend a hand. Our support team doesn't know what to do so they sit on the sidelines waiting for directions. Every time you downplay who you are, reducing what you are experiencing or living through, others decide you don't need their help. They go on with their lives because it doesn't seem like you need their assistance. It's not like they don't have others things to do, but they want to help. They don't want to intrude, interrupt or be conceived as pushy so they do nothing or very little, when in reality they want to be asked for their help.

One way to becoming a better receiver is to practice receiving compliments. Think about when you compliment someone and they deflect your comments or disagree with what you say. If you said, "Your hair looks great today," and they responded with, "No it doesn't, and I didn't get a chance to wash it." You might feel as if they threw your compliment back in your face and might not bother to make the effort next time. If you find yourself making this mistake think about how you respond. Instead graciously say, thank you, even if you don't agree. Realize that most people are genuinely being nice and they believe what they say. Own it. Practice giving and receiving compliments. The more compliments you give the more you will receive, it just works that way. Don't say something you don't believe instead find something you can authentically say. Bring attention to positive attributes you admire or notice.

How do I start giving and receiving compliments?
- Notice positive behavior and say something positive.
- Notice a deed well done and say something positive.
- Notice kindness someone shows you and others, and say something positive.
- Really look at someone, notice the color of their eyes, their smile, etc.
- Be sincere.

When someone gives you a compliment they are giving you a gift. When you don't receive fully the compliment, it's like saying; I don't want your gift. So next time you deflect a compliment, stop and just say thank you and accept the gift being given.

Find Your Courage

When asked to name someone who was courageous, the first person I thought of was Martin Luther King Jr. In my opinion, he epitomizes what I think of as courageous. He stood up for what he believed no matter the circumstances or consequences. He had the guts to say what was right, even if it wasn't popular.

Courage starts with one small act. It may have been the conscious decision to fight the cancer. Now it's the decision to move past the fight and live a life worth remembering. Cancer patients and survivors are courageous. Every one of you is courageous. Whether you get beyond the cancer treatments or have to fight this disease for the rest of your life, that's not the point. It's the idea that we have made a conscious choice to fight and not let cancer beat us today.

Courage is doing the little things that before the diagnosis seemed easy. Like when we get out of bed on those days when it would be so much easier to pull the covers over our head. Get into the shower and start the day, even when in pain, that's courage. Going to all your chemotherapy appointments when you know it will make you feel worse. Going to each and every one of those radiation appointments when you know your skin is red and sore now and is getting worse with each treatment. That's courage.

Courage is picking up one foot after the other and moving forward after treatment. Now it's time to move past the safety nets the treatment and the constant doctor appointments provided. It takes a very brave woman to analyze her life and make the decision that the life she lived before her cancer no longer serves her and does the hard work to move on.

Think of what this world would be like if each of us made one small act that required courage each day. Standing up for what you believe in, giving a voice to the more vulnerable, or creating and acting on ways to improve another's circumstances. We can all be courageous. Start small, but start. You can make a difference in your home, in your neighborhood, in your community, in your world. It can be daunting to think about changing the world, but you can change your world each and every day.

Find the Humor in Life

As we say at Breast Friends, cancer isn't funny but there are a lot of funny moments. Lighten up; laughter improves your outlook, reduces tension and the risk of additional diseases. There are so many things to be serious about, but like a standup comedian, find the little things that go to the extreme and all of a sudden they are funny. I went to a comedy show where the comedian was poking fun at being married and having children. You could tell that he loved being married and being a dad, but like cancer or any other tough challenge you may be facing, there are moments when all you can do is laugh. So find the humor, sometimes it's a stretch but it's worth it.

One patient told me this story. *"I used to think that people could laugh at anything odd. Then I thought it wasn't safe to make a joke about an illness. Doing so might be insensitive to the listener. Now I learned you often have two choices in life, you can laugh or cry. There is a time to cry, but laughter can lighten the load and actually help others around you feel more comfortable.*

I will never forget a specific bone scan. A young male technician had me up on the table ready to begin the procedure. He had not asked me to remove my prostheses. ' After years of being disrobed, prodded, marked, and photographed a person loses a lot of inhibitions. So I said 'Am I supposed to do the test with my prosthesis on?' He wasn't sure and went to check. He came back and said. 'No. So I reached in to my pocketed bra, whipped out the prosthesis and handed him my Jell-O like Boob. I will never forget his look of shock and embarrassment. He carefully cupped the detached counterfeit breast in both hands and walked to the nearest chair and gently set it down. By this time I had to turn my head away to hide my laughter."

Laughter has all sorts of positive effects on the body. Focus on the benefits of laughter. This concept began with Norman Cousins in his memoir, *Anatomy of an Illness,* Cousins, had ankylosing spondylitis, a painful spine condition. He explained that watching comedies like Marx Brothers films and episodes of Candid Camera helped him feel better. Ten minutes of laughter allowed him two hours of pain-free sleep. Recent research confirm the benefits of laughter. The blood vessels of people watching comedy expand and contract easily while the blood vessels of people watching drama constrict, restricting blood flow. In people with diabetes, watching comedy rather than a tedious lecture after eating, results in lower blood sugar. Humor can also raise levels of infection-fighting antibodies and boost levels of our immune cells.

Chapter 11

Goals are Dreams with a Deadline

Linda found her life so affected by cancer she went back to school to become a breast cancer social worker and plans to use her first-hand knowledge to help others who are diagnosed and going through this familiar journey. *"Prior to surgery my mortality was at the center of my mind. My faith became stronger because of this journey. I've decided to be a mentor for other breast cancer patients. My plastic surgeon and I are talking about me working for him after I earn my MSW as a breast cancer social worker. This would be my dream job."*

Linda now has a clear picture of what she wants to do in the future. Not all of us have that clarity.

GPS (Get Planning Something) or Someday

I love my GPS navigation system on my phone. I plug in an address and it starts giving me directions step by step to get wherever it is I want to go. I travel to a place down the street or across country. It can tell me the traffic is slow and give me a few alternatives if I want to avoid freeways or I want the fasted route. What a fabulous tool for my life. Even as wonderful as that device is, I still need to tell it where I am going. I need to know what I want and when I want to get there otherwise it is a useless tool.

That got me thinking how life is like that too. If I don't know where I am going, I don't have the first steps out of my driveway. For most people that means we will do the same things we did yesterday, last week or last year. I need to have a goal in mind; a destination and then I can come up with the plan with the help of my device. As in life, we have been given tools like I have given you in this book, to help you find your destinations, the goals that are important to you and can move you forward. No matter how good the tools, it first takes the desire to go somewhere and then the decision to go now. So let's commit to GPS (get planning something).

"Tell me, what is it you plan to do with your one wild and precious life?" — Mary Oliver, *poet*

Before creating a list of things you want to accomplish, it's imperative to understand what's really important.

Values? What Are They?

Values are those beliefs that are important to us. God, Family, Country are only a few, but when you look at your values, it's important not to parrot what you learned growing up, or what society expects from you. It's time to look deep within yourself and assess what is really important to you. It sounds like an easy exercise but it is the cornerstone of choices you will make in the future. The tricky part is to listen to that inner voice.

I lived the first part of my life trying to fulfill what I thought I was supposed to value. When we experience a midlife crisis, sometimes our value system is right in the middle of the turmoil. For instance, if you went to college because that's what your family wanted. Perhaps you studied what would make you money or you followed in your family's footsteps. However, one day, after this cancer journey or at another crossroads you woke up to realize you don't enjoy what you are doing, this becomes the crisis. So values are important, they drive our behavior, our choices and ultimately our level of happiness.

A personal example: I'm a Christian and I've always been taught that I'm supposed to put God in #1 position, right? In reality when I look at my personal values I put my family above God when I rank them and I'm being honest with myself. God is in the top ten certainly, but I felt guilty to admit He wasn't always #1 on my list. When you look at the time and energy I put into my family vs God, this shows me what's more important. What happens when we say something is important and we don't actually spend our time, money and energy on it, it then becomes an inner conflict. It takes an emotional toll when our values and our actions don't match. This is a great example of the importance of assessing values and living what is truly important to each one of us. If we don't resolve these inner conflicts our happiness level is affected. When our values don't coincide with how we spend our time, something needs to change.

In Appendix 3, take a few minutes and finish this assessment. [33] Look through the long list of words and pick only ten of them as the most important. I know this is difficult, because they all appear important. Think about how you spend your time and energy now or better yet how you want to spend your time and energy in the future, but limit your list to only ten. Some of the words seem similar but they aren't the same. There is no right or wrong answer, just be honest with yourself. There are nuances to each, pick the ones that most speak to you right now.

After you have chosen ten of the value words, rank them from 1 to 10, 1 being the most important, and 10 less important. Since these are your top 10 important values, discern what is the most important and so on. Don't labor

---

[33] Appendix 3

on this, sometimes the first thing that comes into your mind is the best, at least right now. Remember our values shift throughout the years. For instance, when my children were young they were the most important things in my life. Now that they are grown they are certainly still in the top 10 but have slipped down the list and are replaced with other things like adventure that I didn't have time for in the past.

Now look at your list of ten one more time and rank how they actually show up in your life. For instance, if God is #1 in your thinking, but because of work, friends and family obligations He slips to #4 in reality jot that down. Perhaps some thought or conversation needs to happen to either create the time for Him to be #1 or rethink the positioning. Be real, be truthful.

This assessment can be taken many times and it can become a window into what you believe is important and how that compares with your reality. I suggest re-assessing values about every six months to take the temperature of your life.

The most important part of this exercise is to evaluate the life you are living and make sure it aligns with the values you hold dear. If for instance you value your family more than anything on this list, but you don't spend quality time with your parents, your children or your partner, you won't feel fulfilled, happy, or joyful. If contribution is paramount and all you do is work at a job that pays the bills but doesn't allow you to feel you are making a difference, your life won't be fulfilling.

Create a list and clarify your values so all activities can be measured by those values. Commit to the practice of your values. Ask for feedback from others that you can trust. Not everyone is worthy of your trust, so pick those who are trustworthy. Practice living your values when life is easy and when it's hard.

Values are defined by what we spend our time and our money so pay attention to these measurements. If you decide adventure is important but you continue to say you can't afford to travel, it is either not really important or you spend money on less priority items. Listen to yourself as to what's important and compare it to your actions.

"We generally change ourselves for one of two reasons: inspiration or desperation." -- Jim Rohn

Small Steps I Can Take Today

- Have a clear picture of what you want in the future.
- Work on the most important tasks first.
- Everything is a habit, even disorganization. You can change the things you don't like or no longer serve you.

Self-reflection is an important key to change and moving forward. Planning is essential but the *implementation* of the plan is where movement happens. Stop looking in the rear view mirror to see who or where you were. Proactive people do not allow themselves to become victims of circumstances, instead they cause action. Truly successful people understand that goals are simply dreams with a deadline.

Look at life like a map of the United States. If you desire to drive across country, where do you start? Where do I want to end and how much time do I need to make this drive? It would be helpful to research what special points of interests on your travels and then draw out the entire trip in detail. This plan or map resembles long and short term goals. Most people spend more time planning their vacation than they do on their lives.

Even the best laid plans need to be changed if construction causes delays, or detours happen. So keep focused on the ultimate destination and be flexible. Short term goals need to be mapped out too, with shorter time frames and less steps to complete.

One exercise to help map out your life is to write a detail description of your life in the future, say ten years out. A little imagination may be needed. Where will you be living? What is going on with family members? What kind of work are you doing? What kind of hobbies are you enjoying? Describe your life in detail, from friends, work, and family.

Now let's create an alternative ending to your story, really use your imagination and add the flairs that you want to make that life more interesting, more fun, closer to the person you have always wanted to be. Imagine yourself in this life. If you are retired in ten years, what are you doing with your time? If you want to travel, where do you see yourself going and with whom? Are you enjoying the company of new friends, old friends? Look at all aspects of your life, and put the fun, excitement and passion back into the equation.

Now with a better idea of what's important and this creative writing assignment mapping out the next ten years, look for the gaps. Where are you now vs where you want to be in ten years. This is where the goals come into play. Creating a set of goals that will give you the plan needed to get from here to there. The next ten years will fly by, just like the last ten have. Take control of your future by living it and don't let it just slip away.

When setting either long term or short term goals, be specific about what you want to accomplish. Answer the questions like who, when, where, and how to help with this process. Make your goals S.M.A.R.T., [34] Specific, Measurable, Achievable, Relevant, and Timed. This next chapter in your life can be the most fun and exciting if you plan for it to be fun and exciting.

---

[34] Appendix 5

S.M.A.R.T. goals are designed to better identify what you want to accomplish and the steps needed to get there. They will help alleviate the challenges on the journey. S.M.A.R.T. goals are imperative to accomplish your individual benchmarks, and are used by many corporations to evaluate progress.

Create at least three short term goals,[35] and three long term goals.[36] These worksheets help reduce the feeling of overwhelm at the beginning of a project. They give you the directions, the map needed to get to your destination.

If you want to experience Europe in the next ten years, you will need to start planning the trip. The long term goal may be: Travel to five countries in Europe by summer of 2020. There are many shorter term or lesser goals needed to accomplish this amazing trip. You will need a passport. You'll need to create a travel budget, save money, pick a date, buy your tickets etc. I've created both a long term and short term goal worksheet to help you in your goals setting efforts.

"No one can go back and make a new beginning but anyone can change and make a new ending." Jim Rohn

Significant and Meaningful

One of things I realized after enduring the cancer experience was small talk was more difficult for me. It completely bores me. The idle chitchat that is meaningless. To me it feels amazing to talk about matters that are significant and meaningful rather than shallow and trite. After looking at my mortality I found power I never knew I had. I was able to realize an inner strength that has always been there, but I hadn't tapped into it until I took the focus

---

[35] Appendix 6
[36] Appendix 7

off myself and let it shine elsewhere. It was necessary to reach down deep into my character and learn to rely on God and my own strength to be the person I was designed to be.

My journey through breast cancer allowed me to find my passion and, in turn, help others to find theirs. It has made it possible to get beyond old negative feelings, restore my spirit so I'm open to new adventures and embrace all aspects of my life. I am able to objectively assess and embrace the positive parts of my life and rid myself of the rest. Breast cancer has allowed me to discover who I really am, and what God put me on this earth to do. Breast Friends is my vehicle to being the best I can be, thriving by sharing and caring for others. I have the opportunity to help women move from patient to survivor, and then to thriver. What more can I ask?

So this can be your reality too. Find what you are designed to do on this earth in the short time we have. To use this experience to make yourself a better person, to talk about the aspects of life that matters. To help others in ways that will leave a lasting impression and inspire those that you touch.

Embrace what is, even if it isn't the way you envisioned this portion of your life, and again look for the small wins. Maybe your disease is back, but it has been caught early so it can be managed. Live intentionally rather than just floating through life. Choose your path, rather than allowing it to choose you.

Get moving toward living and new goals. Regardless of your situation, create goals, things you want to do, places you want to see, things you want to experience. Meet new friends, experience new foods, find new hobbies. Not everyone wants to travel, but perhaps your own backyard maybe a little slice of heaven. Enjoy that backyard, garden, and invite friends over to enjoy the beauty. We all have stories; no one gets through life without tragedy shame, struggles and traumas. Only you have the power to make your life what it is meant to be. Live Life.

"Everything can be taken from a man but one thing: the last of the human freedoms—to choose one's attitude in any given set of circumstances, to choose one's own way."

Viktor E. Frankl, Man's Search for Meaning

The End

About the Author

Sharon is a 24 year breast cancer survivor and uses her experience to demonstrate compassion, thoughtfulness and caring for those whose lives have been touched by this disease. She wrote *Thriving Beyond Cancer* to provide hope and inspiration to any woman facing her biggest challenge.

Determined to spare other women the unnecessary trauma of her own experience, Sharon co-founded Breast Friends, an Oregon grassroots non-profit organization founded in 2000, to "help women survive the trauma of cancer one friend at a time."

An integral part of Breast Friends, Sharon continually creates, implements and facilitates programs designed to relieve the suffering and emotional journey of patients undergoing treatment and help breast cancer survivors to thrive. Breast Friends also provides emotional support for patient families, helping them cope with the emotional upheaval cancer brings to everyone's lives. Over the past 20 years, Sharon has offered hope and inspiration to thousands of families. Her mission is always to provide women with the tools they need to move on and thrive after cancer.

In addition to her work with cancer survivors, Sharon provides the tools of self-esteem, confidence, and inner power to women of all ages. She has volunteered at the women's Coffee Creek Correctional Facility for 10 years and delivered her self-esteem workshop to 40 – 50 prisoners each month for the last four years. Her compassionate coaching style enables women to feel comfortable and learn to dream, perhaps for the first time. She helps them identify what's important to them, set appropriate boundaries, and create a plan that will lead them to a better quality of life.

Sharon further enriches people's lives with her love of self-improvement and is a personal Certified Life Coach to many. She is a masterful knitter, jewelry maker, and an extraordinary hostess. In her spare time, she also loves to explore any nook and cranny to find just the right angle to photograph.

Bring Thriving Beyond Workshop to Your Community

Breast Friends wants to partner with your hospital or clinics to bring this effective survivorship program to patients who have finished the formal part of the treatment. Thriving Beyond is a two day workshop for women have the desire to move forward. Sharon Henifin has been facilitating these workshops and retreats since 2009. The key areas of Survivorship including but not limited to:

- Overcoming Fear, Positive Psychology-Self-Talk
- Life Balance, Setting Priorities
- Coping Skills, Life Planning
- Achieving Your Dreams

You can reach Sharon Henifin at 503-598-8048 or sharon@breastfriends.org for more information about bringing Thriving Beyond to your community.

I want to thank all the ladies who have shared their lives with me and who have taught me the importance of the work I do. I appreciate the women who have allowed me to use their words to demonstrate how all of our journeys are different but yet, very much the same.

I want to thank all who helped me write and edit this book, without you it would be still a dream. With special thanks to Michelle Cameron, without her this book may not have been possible.

Contributor

Michelle Cameron , MD, PT, MCR who has authored over 35 peer reviewed papers, over 50 invited reviews, and three textbooks, one of which is a best seller in its field. Dr. Cameron helps keep the medical facts accurate and the writing clear and directed. We are excited to publish this book as a tool for women to get beyond cancer and go on to have their best lives after cancer.

If you are interested in connecting with me, I can be reached at sharon@breastfriends.org. I am available to do one on one coaching, workshops and retreats.
Sharon Henifin CLC, CN-BA

Appendix 1

Write <u>20 Positive Words or Phrases</u> that best describe you.

1. _____
2. _____
3. _____
4. _____
5. _____
6. _____
7. _____
8. _____
9. _____
10. _____
11. _____
12. _____
13. _____
14. _____
15. _____
16. _____
17. _____
18. _____
19. _____
20. _____

Appendix #2

Your thoughts and words are vital for positive self-esteem and personal growth. Use the "I Am" phrases below to best describe the person you are and **or want to be.**

I am ambitious	I am loyal
I am authentic	I am optimistic
I am beautiful	I am organized
I am clear	I am passionate
I am coachable	I am patient
I am committed	I am peaceful
I am complete	I am personable
I am competent	I am proactive
I am confident	I am professional
I am courageous	I am progressive
I am creative	I am reliable
I am dependable	I am resourceful
I am developing	I am respectful
I am disciplined	I am responsible
I am efficient	I am satisfied
I am empowered	I am secure
I am faithful	I am strong
I am flexible	I am successful
I am friendly	I am supportive
I am fulfilled	I am talented
I am generous	I am trustworthy
I am gifted	I am unique
I am happy	I am wise
I am healthy	I am making a difference
I am honest	I am innovative
I am imaginative	I am loving
I am enough	I am independent

Appendix #3
Value Assessment

	Put a checkmark beside the ten values you hold most strongly.	2) Rank these ten in order of importance to you. (1=most, 10=least)	3) Then rank the ten you chose by how often they show up in your life. (1=most, 10=least)
achievement			
adventure			
balance			
beauty			
children			
commitment			
community			
communication			
competition			
contribution			
creativity			(
education			
empowerment			
excellence			
family			
freedom			
friendship			
fun			
God			
happiness			
health/fitness			
honesty			
independence			
integrity			

intimacy			
job/career			
leisure			
love			
loyalty			
marriage			
money			
nature			
peace			
pleasure			
recognition			
romance			
security			
self-confidence			
self-expression			
self-improvement			
solitude			
spirituality			
trust			
wholeness			
wisdom			

Appendix #4
Passion

Principles- Our core values differentiate you from me.
- What do you invest your time and money now?
- Are these activities that you value most?

Attitudes- The way you think about yourself and others.
- What positive or negative actions and behaviors shape your life?
- What are the defeating thoughts and self-talk inside your head that no one hears?

Strengths- The things you enjoy and are naturally good.
- What do people like about you?
- What natural abilities make you a unique person?

Skills- Those abilities you've been able to learn.
- What skills come easily?
- What activities can you best use these skills?

Identity- Roles we play and what they mean.
- What aspects of yourself do you love?
- What aspects of yourself would you like to chance?

Opportunities- The growth prospects we are faced with.
- What opportunities are you ready for when they present themselves?
- What is holding you back from seeking change?

New Life- Combining your passion with your strengths.
- What does your new life look like?
- When will you embrace this new life?

Appendix #5
Goal Setting

Goals are most effective when written down and are stated in a positive statement.

Break goals into bite size pieces so they can be accomplished more easily and you can see your forward movement. If a goal is too large, it may look too daunting to set you up to fail.

Use the SMART mnemonic; it can help you remember the components that make an effective goal.

Specific
Measurable
Attainable
Realistic
Timely

Practice writing one goal using SMART.

_____

_____

_____

_____

_____

_____

_____

Appendix #6

Short Term Goal Development

Life Balance Components:
☐ Emotional ☐ Mental ☐ Physical ☐ Spiritual
☐ Financial ☐ Career ☐ Social ☐ Relationship

Short Term Goal:

Desired Date of Achievement:

Please copy extra sheets

Small purposeful steps to get to your goal

Task	By When	Step #	✔

Appendix #7

Long Term Goal Development

Life Balance Components:
❐ Emotional ❐ Mental ❐ Physical ❐ Spiritual
❐ Financial ❐ Career ❐ Social ❐ Relationship

Long-Term Goal:

Desired Date of Achievement:

Please copy extra sheets
Small purposeful steps to get to your goal

Task	By When	Step #	✔

Appendix #8
Living a Life of Purpose

What four goals will you fulfill in the following areas of your life in the next five years?

Relationship/Family

1. _____
2. _____
3. _____
4. _____

Spiritual

1. _____
2. _____
3. _____
4. _____

Physical/Health

1. _____
2. _____
3. _____
4. _____

Mental

1. _____
2. _____
3. _____
4. _____

Living a Life of Purpose (continued)

Emotional

1. _____
2. _____
3. _____
4. _____

Social

1. _____
2. _____
3. _____
4. _____

Financial

1. _____
2. _____
3. _____
4. _____

Job/Career

1. _____
2. _____
3. _____
4. _____

Made in the USA
Columbia, SC
28 January 2018